HEROES C
THE RAF

No 50 SQUADRON

Rupert Matthews

Bretwalda Books Ltd

First Published 2012
Copyright © Rupert Matthews 2012

Bretwalda Books
Unit 8, Fir Tree Close, Epsom,
Surrey KT17 3LD

info@BretwaldaBooks.com

To receive an e-catalogue of our complete
range of books send an email to
info@BretwaldaBooks.com

ISBN 978-1-907791-27-7

Bretwalda Books Ltd

Introduction

I came to Dover to look for the remains of the World War II radar station that stood on Swingate Down and was known as CH04. I knew that much of the radar station had been dismantled in the 1950s, but that the main mast had been retained and converted to broadcast BBC radio stations across Kent and the English Channel.

NO 50 SQUADRON CREST
The squadron crest shows a sword cutting through a cloak and refers St Martin who cut his cloak in half to share with a beggar.

It took a bit of nosing about, but I eventually found the place. It was not until I got there and read the information board that I realised that CH04 had been built on the site of an earlier airfield that had been used by the RAF in the 1920s, and before then by the RFC in World War I. I made a note of the fact, and decided to look into this RFC airfield another time. Some while later, I had the opportunity to investigate RFC Swingate Down. It had been opened in 1914 to serve as a stop for refuelling aircraft on their way out to France, and then used for training purposes.

So far so good. But what intrigued me was that in the summer of 1916 the airfield at Swingate Down was recorded as having been the home base for a squadron of scouts (as fighter aircraft were then known) – and that the squadron in question had been No.50 Squadron. What puzzled me was that I knew that in World War II No.50 Squadron had been a heavy bomber squadron. Yet here it was in 1916 as a fighter squadron. Not only that but a little further research turned up the name of the squadron's commanding officer: Major Arthur Harris.

So not only had one of World War II's premier bomber squadrons been a fighter unit in World War I, but the great and famous Arthur "Bomber" Harris had been a fighter pilot. I was now thoroughly hooked. No.50 Squadron, its men and machines became a focus of research for me. And this book is the result.

WAITING, 1940
Ground staff at an RAF bomber base "somewhere in England" await the return of their aircraft from a raid on Germany in 1940. The author's father served as one such man tasked with counting the aircraft as they returned.

5

The
Great War

In the spring of 1916 Britain had a serious, terrifying and devastating airborne problem. No.50 Squadron was created to face up to that menace from the air, and to destroy it. That the squadron did its job cannot be doubted, for within months the terror was gone – though only to be replaced by one even more destructive. And No.50 Squadron was hurled into the struggle to defeat that new devilish weapon.

The night time terror from the skies came in the form of gigantic Zeppelin airships that cruised over the North Sea from Germany laden with bombs that their crews dropped with often devastating accuracy on towns, cities and ports across eastern Britain. The first raid had come in January 1915 when Great Yarmouth and King's Lynn were bombed by night. Four people were killed, 16 injured and property worth £8,000 was destroyed. Over the following months dozens of raids were carried out by the Zeppelins, killing 181 people, wounding 455 and causing almost a million pounds worth of damage. Clearly something had to be done to stop the menace.

The problem was that the Zeppelins flew high, at the very ceiling of contemporary fixed wing aircraft. And while they were huge, the parts of them that were vulnerable were remarkably small. A few bullet holes in the gas bags that made up the bulk of the craft made little difference to their bouyancy. The engines and the crew, together with their bombs and machine guns, were housed in gondolas slung underneath the vast gas bags. Anti aircraft artillery could certainly do damage, and were thought capable of bringing down a Zeppelin, but again the height of the airships made hitting them from the ground difficult. In any case the German raiders came at night. Searchlights might reach the Zeppelins to illuminate them for the gunners on clear nights, but were ineffective on cloudy nights. Not so the raiders. They lowered men in observation cars that dangled 3,000 feet or more below the Zeppelin to telephone messages back up to the gondola to tell the pilot where to steer and the bomber when to drop his deadly load.

In February 1916 the air defence of Britain was handed over to the army, which gave the task to the Royal Flying Corps (RFC), then part of the army. The RFC decided that anti aircraft guns with searchlights were the best nocturnal defence and drew up plans for hundreds of combined gun-light batteries to be installed round cities and towns. During daylight hours, trust was placed in the new models of scout aircraft entering service that could climb up to the operating height of the Zeppelins fast enough to stand a

ZEPPELIN SPY BASKET, 1916
These precarious capsules were lowered through cloud on a wire from a Zeppelin. A man inside telephoned back to the airship a description of what he could see to help with navigation and bombing.

B.E.2C ROYAL AIRCRAFT FACTORY, 1916
The B.E.2 entered service in 1912, with the C
version being produced from 1914. It remained in
service to the end of the Great War, though by 1918
was used only as a trainer.

chance of catching them. The RFC formed a number of Home Defence
Squadrons, mostly based on the east coast or near London, which were tasked
with tackling any Zeppelins which came in sight during daylight hours, for
even with mounting attacks by night - night flying by planes was always
hazardous business at this date.

And so, on 15 April 1916, the Royal Flying Corps brought into existence
No.50 Squadron, tasked with home defence against Zeppelin airships. The
squadron was called into existence at Swingate Down, a small airfield perched
high on the hills northeast of Dover, Kent. Swingate Down was not much of
an airfield. The smooth grass of the chalk downs provided a good enough
runway, but the only buildings were a scattering of wooden huts and a couple
of wooden hangars.

The RFC had been using the place as a refuelling stop for aircraft flying out to France. There was enough accommodation for the men tasked with the refuelling, and a bed or two for pilots forced to stay overnight by bad weather – and that was about it. The arrival of a full squadron put a severe strain on the base at Swingate Down, which was met by more wooden huts and a number of tents. Fortunately the summer of 1916 was kind so far as weather was concerned.

Less kind to No.50 Squadron were the aircraft with which they had been equipped. These consisted of a number of B.E.2c and B.E.12 scouts, neither of which were really up the job in hand. The B.E.2c was a slightly updated variant of the B.E.2 which had entered service in 1912 and which in 1914 had proved to be an effective reconnaissance aircraft. It had been designed by the famed air engineer Geoffrey DeHavilland and sported the distinctive teardrop shaped tail fin that he favoured. It could remain in the air for over 3 hours, then a useful endurance for a scout, but its top speed of only 72 mph and armament of a single .303in machine gun (facing backward and operated by the observer) meant that by 1915 it had been outclassed as a fighter.

The B.E.12 was another DeHavilland design, and was essentially an upgraded B.E.2c. It could reach 102mph and had a forward firing machine gun as well as the rearward firing one. With its 3 hour endurance and good rate of climb, the B.E.12 was reckoned to be an effective answer to the

ZEPPELIN GUNNERS, 1916
A contemporary illustration showing German gunners mounted on the top of a Zeppelin firing machine guns at British nightfighters, such as those of No.50 squadron, while searchlights from the ground seek out the Zeppelin.

Zeppelin problem. It was an inherently stable aircraft, which made flying at night safer, while its endurance in the air gave the pilot plenty of time to find his airfield - or some other convenient open space - on which to land after combat. Like the B.E.2c, however, it was already outclassed by other aircraft as a fighter. However, the more modern and more nimble models were needed in France to tackle German fighters, so the B.E.12 was given to the Home Defence Squadrons.

The men of No.50 Squadron spent their first few weeks settling in and flying patrols out over the Dover Straits. Zeppelin raids took place over East Anglia and the Northeast, but no great airship came anywhere near Swingate Down.

Then, a little after 2am on the morning of 25 August a phone call came in from the Fire Brigade in Folkestone. Air engines could be heard over the sea to the east and, given the slow speed at which the engines seemed to be moving, they were almost certainly those of a Zeppelin. The squadron raced

VICKERS E.S.1, 1916
No.50 Squadron was the only unit ever to fly this fighter in combat. At 118 mph the fighter was very fast for 1915, but the design of the upper wing blocked the view of the pilot so the model was never put into production.

to its action stations. At 2.15am the Zeppelin passed over Folkestone harbour heading northeast. A searchlight near Dawkinge Wood managed to get its beam on the intruder, at which the anti aircraft guns of Folkestone opened fire. The sudden barrage of noise awoke the entire town and people poured into the streets to gaze upward at the ghostly white behemoth overhead. None of the exploding shells hit the Zeppelin, which then turned slightly south and moved out of range of the searchlight, causing the guns to fall silent. The unnamed man writing up the official record in the nightwatch book at Folkestone Fire Station thought that the Zeppelin "crew were probably endeavouring to baffle the gunners on the hills."

In fact, the Zeppelin was doing nothing of the sort. The airship was LZ32 commanded by Oberleutnant-zur-See Werner Peterson, who had spent some time that night lost. He had now identified the town beneath him as Folkestone and thus knew that the great port of Dover, one of his targets, was only a short distance away. He was now heading for Dover, the change in course having been made necessary by a shift in the wind at altitude.

Meanwhile, No.50 Squadron was in the air and making for the scene of action. When the searchlight went out they had to rely on the faint starlight for guidance. There was quite a lot of cloud about and most pilots lost the airship among the clouds. One B.E.2c, however, found the LZ32. The pilot flew alongside while his observer poured his entire stock of bullets into the great airship. The hail of fire had no discernable impact on the Zeppelin, which continued on its course to Dover. Arriving over Dover, Peterson dropped his bombs on the harbour, and ships anchored outside, hoping to hit the various naval ships moored there. He failed to hit a single one, though there were some near misses.

Next day an official communique was issued by the German government to the pressmen from neutral countries in Berlin. It read:

"During the night of August 24-25 several naval dirigibles attacked the southern portion of the East Coast of England. They dropped numerous bombs on the City and the South Eastern district of London and the batteries at the naval stations at Harwich and Folkestone, and numerous vessels moored in Dover Harbour. Everywhere very good results were observed."

The attack on the City of London had been real enough. LZ31 had bombed a wide area, killing 9 people, injuring 40 and inflicting £130,000 of damage. The claimed damage on Folkestone and Dover was, however, imaginary.

The excitement over, No.50 Squadron settled back into its routine of patrols and a lack of any real action. The fact that the No.50 crew had emptied their entire stock of ammunition into a Zeppelin without inflicting damage was reported back to RFC headquarters, where it caused some consternation. It was known that the airships were filled with highly inflammable hydrogen, which being much lighter than air gave them their lift. It had been assumed that bullets would tear a hole in the gas bags, allowing oxygen to mix with the hydrogen. This mix would then be ignited by the heat of the bullets, or sparks caused by them hitting the metal framework, and the airship would explode. This had not happened, and thus a divide opened up among the planners at the RFC. Some thought that the Germans must have encased the hydrogen bags in bags of some inert gas, thus stopping oxygen gaining access along with the bullets.

Others thought that bullets alone were not enough to ignite the hydrogen and urged the adoption of special incendiary bullets. Such ammunition was forbidden under international treaty, except when used against particular targets. Pilots carrying such ammunition had to carry a written order signed by a senior officer specifying the target, and were not allowed to open fire on anything else. Any pilot who came down behind enemy lines in an aircraft carrying incendiary ammunition but without a signed order could be shot for war crimes. The use of this ammunition was, therefore, highly controversial. Nevertheless it was eventually introduced to Home Defence Squadrons tasked with attacking Zeppelins.

None of the pilots of No.50 got to use the incendiaries in anger, however, as they never again got within firing range of a Zeppelin. In October 1916 the squadron moved to Harrietsham, on the North Downs near Maidstone, where they were to stay for nearly two years. At Harrietsham the squadron gained a number of new aircraft. Perhaps the most unusual of these was the Vickers E.S.1, of which only three were ever built and only this one entered operational service. This Experimental Scout was very fast for its day, but due to a problem with its centre of gravity the pilot's seat was placed under the upper wing. This meant he could see very little, a fatal flaw in a combat aircraft. Rather more successful was the Bristol M.1, the only British monoplane fighter to enter service in World War I. The Bristol M.1 was fast, agile and easy to fly. However it had a high landing speed, which required a long runway. This made it unsuitable for use in the often makeshift airfields of the Western Front, but there was no such problem at Harrietsham.

The squadron also gained a number of R.E.8 two seaters and Armstrong Whitworth F.K.8 two seaters. Both these aircraft were designed to be general purpose machines, able to carry bombs or act as reconnaissance aircraft. They were also light and agile enough to act as escort or long range fighters, though they were not as nimble as the single seat scouts entering service in 1917.

By 1917 the introduction of incendiary bullets had made Zeppelin raids a thing of the past. The Germans had instead introduced the long-range Gotha bombers that had the range to reach London. These now became the main target for No.50 Squadron. The Gotha GIV had entered service in March 1917 with the specific aim of bombing London. The aircraft were large, twin engined bombers that could carry half a ton of bombs. They were each equipped with 3 machine guns mounted so as to give all round defence against enemy fighters – even covering the vulnerable area under the tail of the aircraft.

ANTI AIRCRAFT GUN, 1917
Manned by a naval crew, this anti aircraft gun was positioned to defend London from German aerial attack. The navy was in charge as they had more experience of firing at moving targets than did the army.

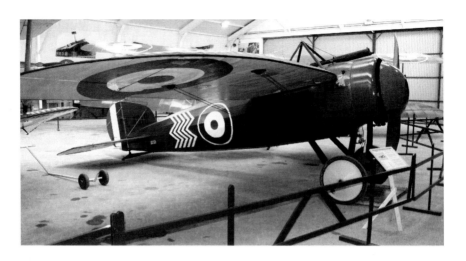

BRISTOL M.1, 1917

The Bristol M.1 was the first British monoplane
fighter. This is a M.1C model with a single machine
gun fitted in front of the pilot. This type was
popular with senior RFC officers who needed a
private aircraft to visit bases under their command.

The first Gotha raid came on 25 May 1917 when Folkestone and
Shorncliffe were bombed causing 95 deaths, 195 injuries and a large amount
of damage to buildings. No Gothas were lost. Further raids followed with no
German losses, but heavy damage inflicted on Britain. The death toll among
civilians rose alarmingly – in one raid a school was hit and 46 children killed.
The British aircraft found that they took a long time to climb to the 15,000
feet height at which the Gothas crossed the coast. By the time the defenders
were at the correct altitude, the raiders had gone.

On 7 July yet another Gotha raid came in off the North Sea at 9.30am,
with 22 of the giant bombers heading up the Thames towards London. As
they came up the river the Gothas were met by a lone Sopwith piloted by
Lt John Young with Air Mechanic C.C. Taylor as his gunner. The Sopwith
attacked, but within seconds was caught in crossfire from the Gothas. The
aircraft broke up and fell into the sea, killing both Young and Taylor – neither
of whose bodies was ever found.

No.50 Squadron had meanwhile taken off from Harrietsham and was climbing for height. Squadron commander, Major C. Butler, believed that by the time his formation had got the required height, the Germans would have completed their bombing of London and be heading back to Germany. He therefore led his men to the skies over the Thames Estuary, where they continued to climb for height over Foulness. This was in the days before aircraft were equipped with radios, so once in the air a pilot was on his own. It was very much up to the airman where he went and how he behaved. On 7 July, the flyers of No.50 Squadron would have received no updates on the position or progress of the Gothas. Instead Butler and his men had to guess which route the Germans might take home and position themselves accordingly. No.50 was not the only squadron in the air that day. The news of the approach of the Gothas had caused men across Kent and Essex to leap into their aircraft. There were now more than 80 British aircraft cruising the skies east of London seeking the Germans.

The Germans, meanwhile, had moved on up the Thames Estuary. Over Dartford they changed course to the northwest, then over Ilford turned southeast. Beneath them large crowds gathered in the streets to watch the formation of large aircraft flying in a perfect triangular formation. The RFC had been issuing statements to the press about their new anti-aircraft guns and the presence of numerous Home Defence Squadrons, and so effective had these statements been that Londoners assumed that no Germans could get to London and so took the Gothas to be British. Not until anti aircraft guns in Stratford opened fire did anyone realise a raid was in progress. At once everyone ran for cover.

Then the bombs fell. The main target was the City of London. One German seemed to aim at the dome of St Paul's Cathedral, but missed and destroyed the post office next door. Another hit an office building at the very moment that 75 typists were fleeing downstairs to the basement, amazingly none were killed though several were wounded. A school yard was hit, killing 8 children and wounding 50 more. In all 59 people were killed and 193 injured. The fact that for the second time in two raids a school had been hit enraged the Londoners. That night and for several subsequent nights there would be riots in which businesses run by immigrants of German descent were destroyed and their owners beaten up. Many people with German-sounding names were taken in protective custody by the police or urged to move out of London.

Meanwhile, at 10.40am, the German aircraft turned around and, still in perfect formation, headed east toward the waiting British scouts. Butler had guessed right, so No.50 Squadron was able to engage the Germans over the Essex coast. Lt Max Cremetti, the son of a famed London art dealer of Italian origin, charged headlong into the German formation. He flew straight through it from end to end while his observer raked the Germans with gunfire. Having completed his run, Cremetti turned around and flew straight back through the Germans a second time.

One of the Gotha's began to fall behind the formation, perhaps with engine trouble. It was spotted by Lt F.A.D. Grace, who zoomed in to the attack. His observer Lt. G. Murray waited until they were at very close range before opening fire. The Gotha began to emit smoke and went into a dive. Not wanting to be cheated, Grace followed it down and saw it crash at full speed into the sea off Harwich. Grace and Murray were flying an Armstrong Whitworth F.K.8, which had a forward firing machine gun operated by Grace as well as rearward firing gun used by Murray.

Butler, meanwhile, had been leading his men in a series of attacks on the German formation. The running fight continued as the Gothas headed out over the North Sea, heading for their base near Zeebrugge. Butler himself saw a Gotha that he attacked go down about 20 miles off Ostend, but could not follow it down as he was busy trying to keep his squadron in formation. Lt R.H. Daly and Lt J.E. Scott attacked a Gotha that they saw going down near Walcheren. In the event, neither of these Gothas was destroyed, though they were both badly damaged and several of their crew members had been killed. Indeed, German losses in terms of killed and wounded - though not in aircraft lost - had been heavy. This was to be the last large daylight raid on London, thereafter the Gothas came at night or made quick hit-and-run raids on coastal targets.

In February 1918, the squadron underwent some important changes. It moved to an airfield at Bekesbourne south of Canterbury. At the same time its odd mixture of aircraft was replaced by a force of S.E.5 scouts. This superlative single seat machine could top 135mph and reach 17,000 feet. It was armed with two forward firing machine guns and soon proved itself to be a highly effective fighter. The pilots also underwent training in night flying and night fighting, ready to tackle the Gothas as they came over at night. The aircraft were painted black to make them difficult for the Germans to spot at night.

One night in May 1918 Lt Colin Packham was sent up in his SE5 to tackle a Gotha that had been heard over Thanet. He climbed for height, then swung east to look for the intruder. Searchlights flickered on over Margate, catching the German bomber and illuminating it clearly. Packham felt confident that he would be able to stalk the German, then shoot it down. As he closed on the Gotha, however, anti aircraft fire suddenly opened up. The shells

CHILDREN FUNERAL, 1917
The East End of London came to a halt for the funeral of the 8 children killed by German bombs in the raid of 7 July. Civilian deaths in warfare were something new for Britain.

GOTHA 4A, 1917
The twin engined Gotha was the main German strategic bomber of the Great War. This is a 4A model with a plywood fuselage and larger fuel tanks than earlier models.

missed the Gotha, but Packham suffered a near miss and his engine caught fire. Packham put his nose down and accelerated, breathing a sigh of relief when the flames went out. Now engineless, Packham glided down to a bumpy crashlanding in Kent. The Gotha cruised on undamaged.

Right at the end of the war, No.50 Squadron acquired a new commanding officer in the form of Major Arthur Harris. He had spent most of 1917 in France, where he shot down five German fighters, and came from No.44 Squadron which he had been commanding in its Home Defence duties. He had recently been awarded the Air Force Cross and came with a reputation for no-nonsense attitudes to discipline. Harris commanded the squadron through the quiet final days of the war when no Gothas came to bomb Britain. It was at this time that the squadron was given the call sign of "Dingo" as radios began to be fitted to aircraft. The squadron's aircraft - by this date Sopwith Camels - were decorated with a picture of a running dog. The running dog would stay with the squadron throughout its subsequent history.

On 13 June 1919 the squadron was disbanded. Most of the men returned to civilian life, though Arthur Harris stayed on in what was by that date the Royal Air Force (RAF). No.50 Squadron was to encounter him again.

Off to War

After 18 years in retirement, No.50 Squadron returned to being on 3 May 1937. It was based at RAF Waddington, near Lincoln, which like No.50 Squadron had been mothballed after the Great War, but was now being returned to service. Amidst the building work of a major bomber base being brought into being, No.50 Squadron took delivery of its Hawker Hind bombers.

HAWKER HIND, 1937
Painted in the glamorous pre-war silver colour scheme this replica Hind shows the two seat configuration and under wing bomb racks inherited from First World War bombers.

The aircraft must have come as something of a disappointment to the men. The biplane Hind was then being phased out of operational service in favour of more modern aircraft. It had a top speed of 186mph and a ceiling of 26,500 feet. These were reasonable figures, but its armament of two machine guns and barely a quarter of a ton of bombs were disappointing. Officially the Hind was a light bomber tasked with attacking battlefield targets in co-operation with the army. However, nobody was in any doubt that the Hind's usefulness in combat was over and the men of No.50 Squadron must have eyed longingly the sleek lines of the Bristol Blenheims, which also operated out of Waddington.

In December 1938 the squadron got rid of the Hind and instead was equipped with the Handley Page Hampden. No.50 Squadron was to fly these bombers for the next three years. The design of the Hampden, and the reason why it was based in Lincolnshire, had much to do with the way that the RAF expected to fight the next war - already by this date assumed to be against Germany.

The British military had been co-operating closely with the French in the later 1930s, as had the two countries' intelligence services. They had come to the conclusion that in the event of a war against Germany the flashpoint would take place in Eastern Europe. It was assumed that a small portion of the German military would be sent to fight in the east, while the bulk invaded France probably by way of Belgium as had happened in 1914. The French and British would advance into Belgium, again as in 1914, seeking to stop the German advance in eastern Belgium around the new and powerful Belgian fortresses at Eben Emael and on the Albert Canal. Once the German invasion was halted, the war would then become an attritional struggle as in 1914 to 1918.

The British and French military believed that they had more aircraft, more tanks, more artillery and more men than did the Germans. They were confident that they could not only halt the expected German offensive, but could also win an attritional conflict. Intelligence reported that support inside Germany for the Nazi regime was widespread, but not very secure. Heavy casualties for small gains were expected to undermine Hitler's popularity leading either to his overthrow or to his seeking a quick compromise peace. When Poland joined the Anglo-French alliance the confidence of the military was boosted even further. Nobody expected Poland to defeat Germany, but her troops were trained to fight in the Polish forests and swamps and so were expected to hold off even the most determined German invasion for anything up to a year.

The RAF laid its plan accordingly. Short range dive bombers, the Fairey Battle, were constructed to work with the army attacking battlefield targets. Medium range Blenheims were designed to operate from bases in France and Belgium to attack targets behind German lines such as railway lines, ammunition dumps and canals. The longer range Wellingtons and Whitleys were based in Britain and tasked with flying missions across the North Sea to bomb German war industries, oil refineries and power stations. The RAF had another and quite distinct task, that of co-operating with the Royal Navy to sink the Germany navy, or at least confine it to base, and thus secure control of the vital shipping lanes.

Of key importance to this naval task was the constant patrolling of the North Sea, the only route by which the German ships could reach the

HANDLEY PAGE HAMPDEN, 1939
The Hampden was a more modern bomber with enclosed cockpit and gun positions and an internal bomb bay, though it lacked the powered gun turrets and bombload that would become usual.

Atlantic. The North Sea had to be mined and surveyed on a frequent and precise basis. For this task the RAF had the Handley Page Hampden. This aircraft had a range of 1,200 miles, which allowed the aircraft to undertake long patrols over the sea. It was unique in being able to carry mines that were specially adapted to be dropped into the sea from the air. The mine dropping missions would later be code named "gardening" and the different mines named after vegetables. The Hampden could also be adapted to carry a torpedo. It was also able to carry up to a ton of bombs. It had a top speed of 265mph, though it cruised at 170mph, and a ceiling of 23,000 feet.

The aircraft was notable for two features. First it was remarkably aerobatic

HAMPDEN BOMBS AND CREW, 1939
A staged publicity photo shows a Hampden, its crew and two of the bombs about to be loaded into the bomb bay. The Hampden could carry 4,000lb of bombs in various configurations.

for a bomber, having the ability to dive, climb, twist and turn more like a fighter than a bomber. Its other key characteristic was its lack of space. The fuselage was only three feet wide inside, and was divided into a front and a rear section by the large bomb bay. The pilot and co-pilot (also the bombaimer and front gunner) sat in tandem in the front of the aircraft. The two gunners sat one above the other mid way along the fuselage, just behind the wings. The two compartments were connected by a tiny crawl corridor that ran above the bombs. This passage was tricky enough to negotiate on the ground, but in flight was considered to be virtually impassable to a man in bulky flying gear.

In 1939 RAF Bomber Command, to which No.50 Squadron belonged, underwent a reorganisation as the prospect of war with Germany came closer. Air Chief Marshal Sir Edgar Ludlow Hewitt divided his Command into five Groups, each under the command of an Air Vice Marshal. No.1 Group was equipped with light bombers ready to be sent to France. No.2 Group had Blenheims and was based in East Anglia. No.3 Group had Wellingtons and was also in East Anglia to attack Germany. No.4 Group had Whitleys and was based in Yorkshire. No.50 Squadron was linked to the other Hampden squadrons and put into No.5 Group, based in Lincolnshire. Put in command of No.5 Group was none other than Arthur Harris, who had led No.50 Squadron in 1918. He was now an Air Vice Marshal and one of the most respected senior commanders in the RAF.

War broke out on 3 September 1939, which found No.50 Squadron already on full alert and ready for action. The plans of the RAF for the air war were, however, thrown off balance early on. Not only was Poland conquered in less than a month, but the French refused point blank to allow any RAF bombers to attack Germany. The French were terrified of what they believed to be huge numbers of German bombers in the Luftwaffe. The French argued that only military targets could be attacked, and then only if there was no risk of civilian casualties. German reprisals, they said, would fall on French cities that lay closer to Germany than did British cities. Attacks on German weapons factories and transport links were therefore impossible.

The men of No.50 Squadron were not as affected by this change as were those of other squadrons. They merely concentrated on their "gardening", or mine laying, missions and on patrolling the North Sea. They also successfully bombed the flare paths used for nocturnal landings by the German seaplanes based in the East Frisian Islands.

At this early date, nobody was entirely certain how long the war was going to last, nor how the men were going to cope with the strain of active service. During the Great War, airmen had stayed with their squadrons until they were needed for training duties, until their commanding officer thought they needed a rest or until they were killed. As the new war opened the same sort of attitude was adopted. The RAF put in place a large scale recruitment and training drive that was intended to produce a mass of new pilots, navigators and gunners, but those men would take a year or more to be ready for combat. In the meantime it was up to the regular airmen to man the squadrons - in many cases continuing to fly until they were killed.

Among the men with No.50 Squadron faced by this daunting prospect was Sergeant Alan Coad, a navigator and co-pilot. He would complete 27 operations as navigator before being promoted to being pilot and captain of his Hampden. After another six operations and a total of 203 operational flying hours he was stood down for a rest in October 1940. A month earlier Sergeant Thomas Cairns had completed 206 hours and 34 missions as a gunner and was likewise stood down. So was Sergeant John Bulcraig, who had completed 210 hours and 34 missions by September 1940 and air gunner Fred Brook with 31 missions by August 1940. Sergeant Alf Bake, another gunner, had completed 32 missions and 212 hours by September 1940 while Sergeant Geoffry Ashmore had served on 30 missions as a gunner by the same date. These men were the lucky ones. Many others had ended their time with No.50 Squadron by being shot down.

While these men flew their long and often fruitless patrols came news that, on 17 March 1940, a German bomber force had attacked the British naval base at Scapa Flow and in so doing injured a few civilians. Churchill authorised a reprisal attack on a German naval base, and the seaplane base of Hoernum on the island of Sylt was selected as the target. No.50 Squadron was one of the squadrons ordered to take part in the raid, scheduled for 19 March. In all 43 bombers made for Sylt, Whitleys as well as Hampdens.

Among the crews going in to attack was that led by Flight Lieutenant James Bennett. He chose to go in at only 1,000 feet in the expectation that he would thus be able to identify the target clearly. As it turned out, it was the Germans who were able to identify his aircraft and even before he reached Sylt Bennett's Hampden had been picked up by a searchlight. Bennet continued to fly straight into the dazzling beam of the intensely bright light, even after a second searchlight found him. He scored a direct hit on the seaplane base, setting fire to what his rear lower gunner identified as a storage hangar. Bennett was awarded the DFC for this exploit, and in 1942 would gain a bar while flying with No.144 Squadron on his second tour of operations.

All the bomber crews claimed to have found their target and to have bombed accurately. The attack began at 8.15pm and continued for more than three hours. Radio messages sent back to base were hurriedly passed on by telephone to Prime Minister Neville Chamberlain in London. At 10pm Chamberlain asked the Speaker in the House of Commons if he could make a short statement. He announced that "Tonight the Royal Air Force attacked and severely damaged the German air base at Hornum on the island of Sylt." He sat down again to have a piece of paper pushed into his hand.

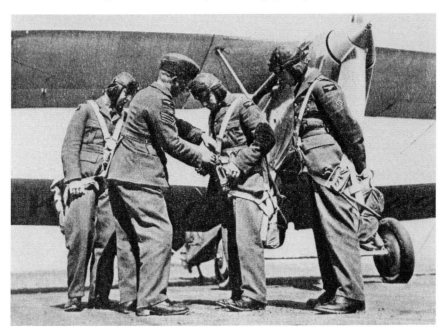

PILOTS TRAINING, 1939
The outbreak of war caused the RAF to begin a massive recruitment and training programme, with aircrew a top priority. It would take months before these men joined units such as No.50 Squadron.

SYLT RECONNAISSANCE, 1940

An RAF reconnaissance photo of the Luftwaffe base at Sylt, taken just before the raid by No.50 Squadron. The airfield buildings and coastline can be seen along with parked aircraft.

Chamberlain read the note, then stood up again to add "I understand that the attack is continuing." Cheering broke out in the House of Commons.

The scale of the damage done was unclear as reconnaissance aircraft were unable to go out to photograph the damage due to poor weather. However, an American journalist managed to find a Danish fisherman who had watched the attack from a distance of about two miles. Both Denmark and the USA were still neutral at this point. The Dane reported almost a hundred large explosions, plus one massive blast that he took to be an ammunition dump detonating.

The raid on Sylt was the largest RAF bomber raid of what would later be known as the Phoney War. That prolonged period of limited military activity came to a sudden end on 9 April 1940 when German troops marched into Denmark, while at the same time German ships and aircraft offloaded an invasion force on the shores of southern Norway. Denmark surrendered in hours, but Norway fought on. The Norwegians had been caught unprepared, but the mountainous territory and the huge length of the country promised that the campaign could be a long one. The RAF decided to intervene by bombing German ships taking part in the invasion.

On 9 April the squadron flew to Bergen to attack the ships that Norwegian sources in the town had reported were landing troops. These ships were the light cruisers Köln and Königsberg, artillery training ship Bremse, transport Karl Peters, two torpedo boats and five motor torpedo boats with 1,900 troops. The men of No.50 Squadron were exceptionally keen to get into action. For months they had been kicking their heels at Waddington, filling in time with training missions and occasional "gardening" trips to drop mines into the North Sea. The chance actually to get to grips with the Germans was very welcome indeed. The long distance to Bergen and back – more than 1,000 miles over open sea – did nothing to dampen spirits.

The mission appeared to be a success. The long flight out had been arduous, and icing on the wings was a problem for some aircraft, but the anticipated low cloud over the target area turned out to be only patchy. If bombing conditions were not ideal, neither were they bad. As was then the custom, the pilots chose their own moment and method of attack. Several reported that their bombs fell close to or among the German ships and men. The attack was pushed home at close quarters by the crews, despite the heavy German anti aircraft fire. Pilot Officer W. Mulloy, bombaimer to Flying Officer Jack French, reported that one of his bombs had scored a direct hit on the stern of a German cruiser. In fact he was mistaken, the bomb had missed but it was an understandable mistake for the cruiser had been hit by a Norwegian artillery shell during the attack. The damaged ship turned out to be the Königsberg. Next day the cruiser was finished off by another squadron of bombers flying out of the Orkneys.

Encouraged by the reports of success at Bergen, the squadron was sent out again, this time to bomb German ships anchored at Kristiansand in southern Norway on 12 April. The Kristiansand Raid turned out to be a disaster. Only one aircraft, the Hampden of Corporal John Wallace, who was flying as wireless operator and gunner, managed to find the target. The Hampden attacked, but its bombs missed.

On the return journey, the Hampdens of No.50 and No.83 Squadrons were flying at a low height when German fighters came into sight. The Germans proved to be a mixed force of nimble Messerschmitt Bf109 single seat fighters and heavier, twin engined Messerschmitt Bf110 fighters. The Bf109s took up positions above the Hampdens, but made no move to attack. The Bf110s, however, came down to fly level with the British bombers. The Bf110s edged ahead of the Hampdens, allowing the machine gun operated by the rear-facing observer of the German aircraft to train on the Hampdens, while the British guns could not be brought to bear in return.

The Germans opened fire, quickly driving the Hampden on the far left of the formation into the sea. The Germans then moved on to the next British bomber in line. Not wanting to share the fate of his comrade, the British pilot pulled up to allow his gunners to have a crack at the Bf110s, but at once the Bf109s dived down to rake the bomber with fire and send it flaming into the sea. Whatever the British tried, the result was the same. One by one they were shot down and destroyed, with no survivors. Six Hampdens were shot down in this way, with the only German casualty being a Bf109 that was hit and badly damaged by the guns of Corporal Wallace, before the German fighters pulled off, short of either fuel or ammunition. The shattered British survivors turned for home.

The agony was not yet over. Several of the remaining bombers were damaged. One was forced to crashland on the sea over 120 miles short of the English coast. Corporal Wallace again sprang into action, transmitting position fixes while his bomber circled the crew of the downed bomber who had scrambled into a rubber dinghy. The men were successfully rescued. No.50 Squadron lost 13 officers and men.

CREW READY TO DEPART, 1940

Taken by a press photographer allowed access to an unspecified bomber base in 1940 this photo shows bomber crews departing on a lorry that will take them to their aircraft for a raid.

Thereafter the new head of Bomber Commander, Sir Charles Portal, refused to allow his men to undertake long range missions except at night. It was a policy that would remain in place for most of the war.

By early May 1940 it was widely expected that a German invasion of France would take place within the next four weeks. A key task of British aircraft was to patrol the area behind the German/Belgian border in search of troop movements, and to watch the German navy, now back at base after the Norwegian invasion, for signs that they too were about to move. Squadron Leader Duncan Good and his crew were engaged on one such mission when

29

BERGEN HAMPDEN CREW RETURN, 1940
The raid on German ships at Bergen carrying invading troops was counted a great success and publicity photos such as this given to the press, though it later transpired the bombing had not been as accurate as at first thought.

they were caught by a searchlight. Seconds later a flak shell exploded inside the cockpit, badly wounding Good and smashing the instrument board. Good managed to wrestle his damaged aircraft out of the searchlight and away from the danger area before he slumped unconscious from loss of blood.

Navigator Pilot Officer Walter Gardiner saw Good collapse and leapt to grab the control stick. He managed to pull Good from the pilot's seat and scrambled in himself, using the intercom to summon one of the rear gunners to come to render first aid. At this stage of the war it was usual for one of the other members of a bomber crew to be a trained, though not always fully qualified, pilot. Gardiner had undergone pilot training, but nothing had prepared him for flying a damaged Hampden across the North Sea without any instruments to help him. Nevertheless he managed to get home across hundreds of miles of sea.

Good later returned to duty with No.50 Squadron with a new crew, but his luck did not hold. On 28 April 1941 his Hampden was shot down and everyone on board was killed. Good and his crew lie buried at Chatelaillon, near Bordeaux.

In June 1940 the squadron moved to RAF Hatfield Woodhouse, soon to be renamed RAF Lindholme. The 400 acre site had been commissioned in 1938 as part of the planned expansion of RAF Bomber Command once the likelihood of war became apparent. No.50 was the first squadron to move in, finding five Type C hangars and stoutly built brick and concrete accommodation in place. The squadron was to have this comfortable billet east of Doncaster all to itself for almost a year until a Canadian squadron moved in to share the base.

The move to Lindholme came at the moment that the German invasion of France finally took place. The unleashed panzers smashed through the French lines near Verdun and poured through the gap. Within days the entire British army and much of the French army was cut off from their supply routes and were being pushed back into an increasingly small pocket around Dunkirk. No.50 Squadron, along with other bomber units, was hurled into the fight to bomb German supply lines and transportation links in Germany itself in an attempt to slow the advancing hordes. These were hectic days for British airmen as they were still learning the tricky arts of combat flying, while facing overwhelming odds against them in the skies.

A typical incident came when a Hampden of No.50 Squadron was returning from a bombing mission and was crossing the German coast at around 15,000 feet. Upper rear gunner Sergeant Leonard Maidment sighted three black dots moving fast above and behind them. By their size and speed they had to be fighters, but they were too distant to identify. The fighters must have seen the Hampden soon after Maidment spotted them for they changed direction toward the Hampden, presumably to identify the bomber. As the fighters came closer, Maidment identified them as being Messerschmitt Bf109. At this date the Bf109 was still something of an unknown quantity. It was known to be fast and agile, but its armament was uncertain. Earlier models had been fitted with two or four 7.9mm machine guns, but reports from combats early in 1940 indicated a heavier armament. In fact the Bf109E model had two 20mm cannon in addition to its 7.9mm machine guns, and the new E3 had three cannon.

Maidment was unaware of this awesome force coming towards him, but the presence of three Bf109 fighters was enough to worry about as it was. The Germans swooped down, but Maidment kept up a running commentary on their movements to his pilot, and a steady stream of bursts of fire toward the Germans. After a while the Germans seemed to lose interest and peeled off.

Whether Maidment had heroically defeated three fighters, or if the Germans had been low on fuel was never clear. As with so many incidents early in the war, the aircrew of No.50 Squadron were still learning their trade.

By the end of June the British army had been evacuated through Dunkirk and France had surrendered, along with Belgium and the Netherlands. Britain was alone. Bomber Command was tasked with attacking German war industries in Germany itself, and with attacking the forces gathering for what was expected to be a German invasion of Britain later that summer.

On 26 August, one of the longest-serving pilots with No.50 Squadron almost lost his life in a raid over Berlin. This was only the second RAF raid on Berlin, which was both heavily defended and a long way from Britain. The number of RAF aircraft taking part was small, but the morale effect of even a few bombs dropped on the German capital was immense. Sergeant Ernest Abbott had been with No.50 Squadron since before the war and had completed 33 missions. In the pre-war RAF, bomber pilots were free both to follow their own route to the target and to decide their own bombing method. It was recognised that each crew had its own strengths, and that the professional airmen of the pre-war RAF could be trusted to make the best decisions for their own crew. Abbott was famous in No.50 Squadron for his liking for making low level attacks, and for preferring to be the first pilot to attack. Whenever he took part in a raid he raced at high speed to the target, then tore in at low level both to ensure accurate bombing and to catch the defenders by surprise. Abbott's technique had proved to be successful time and again, but not over Berlin.

Ordered to attack a specific factory, Abbott as usual hurried to the target and having found it despite the scattered low cloud, went down to just 2,000 feet to make his bombing run. The Hampden ran into a storm of anti-aircraft fire and sustained much damage from splinters and vicious buffetting. Nevertheless, Abbott kept on course and the bombs were dropped accurately. Racing away from Berlin, Abbott decided that the damage to his aircraft was not too bad and set course for home. Over the North Sea, however, one of the engines suddenly cut out and could not be restarted. With the prospect of a watery grave beneath them, Abbott and his crew pinned their faith in their remaining engine and carried on. The Hampden eventually got home safely, and none of the crew were any the worse for their adventure.

It was not just pilots who were attracting notice. Sergeant Bernard Bardega was a rear lower gunner on Hampdens, a particularly cramped and awkward position. He uncomplainingly flew 32 long and arduous missions over the North Sea between September 1939 and August 1940. Bardega was one of those quiet, undemonstrative types who just get on with the job in hand without fuss. It was not until he asked to be retrained as a navigator that the higher authorities noticed him and awarded him a DFM for his service.

As the Battle of Britain raged through the summer and early autumn of 1940, the newspaper headlines were full of tales of fighter pilots tackling vast German formations, often against overwhelming odds. But Bomber Command was doing its share too. Along the coasts of northern France, the Low Countries and Germany there were assembling huge numbers of river barges being converted to carry the German army across the Channel to invade Britain. And large concentrations of troops, panzers and other weaponry were being stockpiled ready for the invasion. No.50 Squadron was just one of the bomber squadrons ordered out time and again to attack these targets and so render the expected German invasion less likely to succeed.

As these attacks progressed one man stood out from the crowd. Sergeant Alan Green took an intense and often very vocal delight in opening fire with his machine gun on lorries, trains, German soldiers and anything else that took his fancy. Not only did he open fire with enthusiasm, but his bursts of fire proved to be highly accurate. Before long he was passing on tips and advice to other gunners about how best to ensure hits on ground targets as the Hampdens raced overhead.

Among the gunners who learned from Green was Sergeant William Horner. His moment came in July when his Hampden was returning from an attack. As it crossed the Dutch coast the bomber was set upon by three German fighters. The Germans closed in, but Horner opened fire and saw bullet strikes on two of the three enemy. The fighters then veered off and abandoned the fight.

In October 1940 the squadron was sent to attack the docks at Hamburg. At this stage in the war targets were still identified precisely and crews left to make their own decisions about when and how to attack. One Hampden that attacked low was hit by flak which knocked out the port engine and sent splinters lancing through the fuselage. The radio ceased to work, so gunner and wireless operator Sergeant Eric Day went to work to try to repair it. Before long the bomber was far out over the North Sea heading for home, but unable to gain height. The pilot ordered everything possible to be thrown out, but Day insisted that the radio go last as he feared they might have to ditch and wanted to report their position. In the end the bomber limped over the coast, and Day finally threw his radio out. Day went on to complete 32 missions on his tour of operations, once suffering mild frostbite while manning his guns in appalling weather over Germany.

In December 1940, by which time the threat of a German invasion had receded, the squadron had attacked many other enemy targets, including Berlin, the squadron took part in the first area-bombing attack on a German industrial centre, in this case Mannheim. The concept of area bombing would prove slow to catch on, though by 1943 it had become the standard tactic of RAF Bomber Command. The idea behind area bombing was simple. An area which contained a number of targets would be selected and then the entire area was made the bombing target, not the individual areas within it.

The reason why the concept was not favoured early in the war was because the theories underpinning the bombing campaign had assumed that precision bombing could be carried out effectively. As its name indicates, precision bombing called for the destruction of individual factories, railway bridges and other legitimate war targets in such a way as to ensure their complete destruction while avoiding damage to nearby civilian buildings. Not only was precision bombing cost effective in terms of bombs dropped, money expended and men or machines lost, but it was politically acceptable in neutral countries. Horror stories of Nazi war crimes of bombing churches, museums and civilians were effective in gaining support in neutral countries for Britain. Such support might be lost if RAF bombers likewise hit churches and museums.

The problem was, however, that the RAF was now bombing at night to avoid unacceptably high casualties. Night bombing was notoriously inaccurate. Even if the pilot found the right target, it was more likely than not that his bombaimer would miss the designated factory and hit civilian housing nearby. Even worse, many pilots thought they had found the target when they were in fact miles away, with the result that their bombaimer hit farm buildings, woods or houses that bore a superficial resemblance to the intended target. Thus neutral support was put at risk while bombs were wasted.

Area bombing made it more likely that a useful target would be hit, that bombs would not be wasted and that entirely innocent targets would be missed. Areas chosen for attack were invariably in or near industrial complexes where several factories or transport links were packed closely together. Civilians living nearby were usually industrial workers who laboured in the

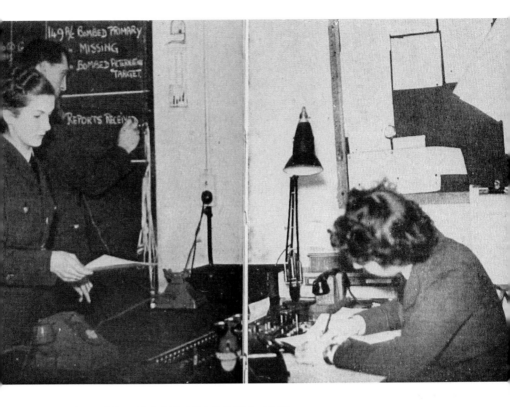

WAAFS IN SQUADRON OPS ROOM, 1940
Women from the Women's Auxiliary Air Force
(WAAF) provided many of the support staff needed
by the RAF. Here WAAFs handle incoming
messages at a bomber squadron operations room.

weapons factories. The RAF could claim with reason that the housing, food
supplies and transport links used by workers in weapons factories were just
as much legitimate war targets as the factories themselves. And if some
workers were killed in the process, nobody in the RAF was going to lose
much sleep after what the Luftwaffe had done to Warsaw, Rotterdam,
Coventry, London and a host of other cities.

At this date, however, most senior RAF officers still had faith in the skills
of their crews to find and hit a target. It would be some time yet before

the RAF abandoned the concept of precision bombing for the vast majority of its raids and adopted area bombing instead. Still more time would elapse before effective means of marking target areas with flares and incendiary bombs were developed to allow less skilled crews to find and hit the correct areas.

The winter of 1940 to 1941 was a tough time for Bomber Command, and for No.50 Squadron. Sir Richard Peirse, who was in charge of Bomber Command, had been ordered to attack oil targets in Germany. Military intelligence believed that Germany was running low on oil and that such attacks would have a great effect on Hitler's war effort. It was later discovered that Germany was actually getting huge amounts of oil from Romania and that the oil attacks were almost pointless. Among the senior commanders who thus lost faith in so-called "panacea targets" chosen by military intelligence was Arthur Harris who thus came to favour area bombing.

The operational problems were made worse by some truly appalling weather that winter that made flying hazardous, even without the interference of the Luftwaffe. One crew that somehow managed to complete every one of the 31 sorties on which they were sent that terrible winter was the crew of No.50 squadron led by Sergeant Raymond Ballantyne. Whether it was luck or skill is unrecorded, but Ballantyne went out and came back having successfully hit the target every single time.

The bad weather could have some interesting results. In February 1941 the squadron was sent out to attack a target in the Ruhr. The aircraft piloted by Sergeant Herbert Crum failed to find the target, but spotted some railway marshalling yards filled with wagons, so Crum went down low to attack those instead. The bombs were dropped, and suddenly the Hampden was hurled upwards by the most massive explosion any of the crew had ever seen. Crum wrestled with the controls to get back control of his aircraft, and then a hurried inspection showed that nothing was badly damaged. Presumably one of the wagons had held ammunition.

Also setting a fine example was Pilot Officer Thomas Burrough who joined the squadron in the autumn of 1940 together with rear gunner Sergeant Alfred Brooks. Over the course of the winter they flew 29 sorties together, totalling 195 hours of operational flying. Burrough displayed what was termed a "cool courage" throughout, while Brooks became a famous joker. In the spring of 1941 Burrough was promoted to be acting Squadron Leader and was awarded a DFC, while Brooks got a DFM.

Some men acquired a reputation for bringing good luck wherever they went. One such as Sergeant Stephen Dawson who joined the squadron in December 1940 along with Flying Officer Vivian Grylls. The pair flew as navigator and pilot, respectively, time and again with Dawson being credited with the luck that brought their Hampden back unscathed from even the most heavily defended targets. A typical example of Dawson's luck came in June 1941, by which time he had risen to be a pilot himself. The target was Kiel and the night was made bright by not only a full moon, but also by unusually active northern lights. The bomber tore over the Danish coast and was at once picked up by the German defences. First one then more searchlights picked up the bomber, and the rear upper gunner reported a Bf110 fighter manoeuvring ready to attack. The gunner turned out to be wrong, there were three Bf110 fighters prowling, not one. Dawson threw the agile Hampden into a series of nervewrackingly violent turns, climbs and dives. Each time the Germans attacked they opened fire with cannon and machine guns, and each time they missed. Despite hundreds of shells and bullets having been fired at his bomber, Dawson's luck held. The machine was entirely undamaged. He went on to bomb the docks at Kiel and got home safely.

Although Britain had been spared invasion in the autumn of 1940 due to the victory of the RAF in the Battle of Britain, all the intelligence reports showed that the Germans were massively increasing the strength of both the Luftwaffe and the army. Opinion was divided as to whether Hitler intended to launch an invasion of Britain in the spring of 1941 or if he might flex Germany's muscles against the states of Eastern Europe. Nobody wanted to take chances, however, so the occupied ports on the far side of the English Channel remained key targets for Bomber Command. Their destruction would make the task of embarking a German army on to ships bound for Britain more difficult.

On 7 February 1941 the squadron was sent to Dunkirk to bomb the docks and shipping. The crew flying with pilot Sergeant Frank Ormanroyd was one of the first of the squadron to go into the attack. He dropped his bombs from just 4,000 feet, watching them burst among buildings on the dockside, two of which caught fire. Realising that other bombers were then coming in to the attack, Ormanroyd went down to 2,000 feet and circled the docks to confuse the defenders, and to allow his gunners to spray bullets at the searchlights. Front gunner Sergeant Edward Roberts was especially keen on

DEBRIEF AFTER RAID, 1940
Bomber aircrew give their
account of a raid to the station's
Intelligence Officer. This debrief
was the first duty of returning
pilots as it gave the RAF a
chance to assess the success of a
raid. It was soon realised that
many pilots gave optimistic
reports.

the task, though it was as a supremely efficient wireless operator that he
attracted notice and for which he was awarded the DFM.

Attacking searchlights was not the preserve of Ormanroyd's crew, several
gunners enjoyed the sport which not only inflicted casualties on the Germans,
but also made the task of flying low at night considerably safer for the
Hampdens. Perhaps the highlight of No.50 Squadron's war on searchlights
came in November 1941 when the bombers were attacking railway yards in
the Ruhr. Sergeant Basil Petrides asked his pilot to circle after dropping the
bombs so that he could "get a good squirt" at the searchlights ringing the
target area. On his first pass, Petrides shot out two searchlights. Encouraged,
the pilot continued to circle and in the next 15 minutes Petrides shot out
another four searchlights. Petrides was to prove to be an enthusiastic exponent
of shooting up ground targets, largely because his pilot favoured flying at low
heights to evade enemy anti aircraft guns. Petrides machine gunned railway
locomotives, goods trucks and lorries whenever he could, once setting a train
of goods wagons on fire.

One pilot who learned at No.50 Squadron the art of low flying to allow
his gunners to shoot up ground targets was Sergeant Alan Quinton. He flew

as co-pilot to Squadron Leader W.R. Russell on eleven sorties during the winter of 1940-41. Quinton later piloted his own Hampden, and continued to prefer low level attack tactics. When attacking targets in the Ruhr he routinely went down below 12,000 feet, and on other targets was often found much lower so that his gunners could attack ground targets as they came in view.

On 21 June 1941 Quinton was on a raid when he was attacked by nightfighters. The aircraft got away safely, but his wireless operator and front gunner, Sergeant Narin Robertson, was badly injured. Robertson was forced off operations, but remained with the squadron and went on to have an adventurous career.

One of the least favourite targets for the crews of Bomber Command was Brest. This huge naval dockyard in occupied France had been taken over by the Germans and for much of the war was used by U-boats and German surface raiders. In January 1941 the pocket battleships Admiral Scheer was at large in the Atlantic sinking merchant ships in large numbers. Military intelligence reported that this warship, wrongly identified as the cruiser Scharnhorst, had put into Brest for maintenance and supplies. On 24 February 1941 No.50 Squadron was sent to Brest to bomb her. As ever the port was very heavily defended. As the Hampdens went in, the aircraft of Flight Sergeant Joseph Hanson suffered a near miss from flak that knocked out one engine. Despite this the bomber completed the attack on the harbour, then limped home on a single engine.

Also on the raid was Flying Officer George Weston. He was determined to hit the target, but arriving over Brest could not see any large warships in dock at all. Putting this down to the light haze drifting in off the sea, Weston circled over the town to give his bombaimer the chance to study the port more carefully. The stooging bomber came in for the attentions of the anti-aircraft gunners and soon it was being bracketed by exploding flak shells. The bombaimer then spotted a large ship and assuming this to be the cruiser Scharnhorst, went down to bomb it.

It was not until a later reconnaissance flight brought back good quality photos that it was realised that Weston had been correct. There had been no large German warships in the port at all, and it was almost a year before the mix up over which raider was at large was sorted out.

On 24 March, the squadron was sent to bomb the naval dockyards at Kiel in northern Germany. Sergeant Ormanroyd repeated the tactics he had used at Dunkirk in February. This time the fire his bombs started grew into a mighty conflagration that his tail gunners reported remained in sight even 10 minutes after the Hampden had left the target area. A month later Ormanroyd and his crew completed their tour of operations having flown 35 missions in 202 hours.

Other targets were easier to find, but much more dangerous to attack. Of no target was this more true than of Berlin. The German capital was a long way from Britain, and much of the route out and back was over enemy occupied Europe where were based Luftwaffe fighters and anti-aircraft guns. The city was itself heavily defended and a dangerous place for RAF crews. In April the squadron was sent to Berlin in one of a series of raids that were designed more to annoy the Germans and remind them that they were at war than to cause any significant damage to the city and its industries. The aircraft piloted by Squadron Leader Goode was flying over the Frisian Islands when it suddenly vibrated to the chatter of the rear lower gun, operated by Sergeant Ray Moore, springing into life.

Barely a second later a cry of triumph came over the intercom from Moore. A flaming ball of fire was seen falling away downwards behind the Hampden. Moore explained that he had spotted a Messerschmitt Bf109 climbing steeply towards them from the rear. Deciding he did not have time to warn the rest of the crew, he had opened fire whereupon the German aircraft had exploded into flames and gone crashing to earth.

In June 1941 the high command at Bomber Command was becoming worried by the apparent lack of success of crews in finding targets. They began experimenting with different tactics to try to increase success. Among these was to detail one crew from a squadron to be the master navigator and target marker. The idea was that the crew with the best navigational record would fly out slightly ahead of the other crews to find the target. Once they had done so, and were absolutely certain they were in the right place, the crew would drop flares and incendiary bombs to "illuminate the target" (the word "mark" was not yet used) for the other crews.

On 12 June No.50 Squadron tried out the new tactic with the Hampden piloted by Sergeant Wilfred Hughes as the designated illuminator. Hughes found the target, railway marshalling yards at Soest, without much difficulty and plastered the area with incendiaries. As he left the target area, Hughes saw bomb bursts and concluded that the rest of the squadron had seen the target by the light of his illuminations and had destroyed it. Only later did it transpire that some crews claimed to have bombed the yards, but said they saw no illuminations. Either they arrived after the fires had gone out, or they had bombed the wrong place. Uncertainty remained.

After the Soest Raid, No.50 Squadron adopted the practice of always bombing from under 15,000 feet in an effort to make target identification easier. It was Sergeant Edward Hunter who led the way in this tactic. He maintained that it was impossible to identify even what city you were over at night from above 15,000 feet. Hunter had begun his career with No.50 as a navigator before being promoted to pilot and so had more of an idea of what he was talking about than did some other pilots. Hunter gradually won the other pilots over to his point of view, and gradually the accuracy of the squadron's bombing improved.

Hunter's crew was generally reckoned to be the best NCO crews the squadron had had to date. The team work between the men was exemplary.

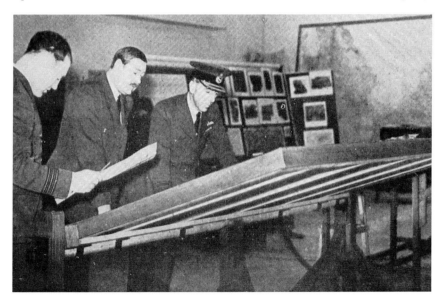

PEIRSE AND BALDWIN AT MAP TABLE, 1940
Air Vice Marshal Richard Peirse (right) and his deputy Jack Baldwin (centre) study a map. Peirse was Air Officer Commanding-in-Chief Bomber Command from October 1940 to January 1942.

When their tour ended in December 1941 the Wireless operator and front gunner Sergeant Richard Newman was awarded a DFM, while Hunter had already been awarded one.

In July 1941 RAF Lindholm was transferred from No.5 Group to No.1 Group, so the squadron moved south to RAF Swinderby just outside Newark, but on the Lincolnshire side of the Trent. One of the last raids flown from Lindholm was a tricky one. The U-boat base at Lorient was in the middle of a populous French town and although the destruction of the base was a high priority, the need to minimise French casualties made it a difficult target to attack. The night of the full moon in July was chosen for the attack and squadrons asked to send their best low-flying crews to take part. Among the crews sent from No.50 was that of Sergeant Stanley Willett. Willett bombed from a height of 1,500 feet, his bombs straddling the docks, but he only just managed to escape the deadly trailing cables of the barrage balloons that

---

MESSERSCHMITT BF110, 1940

Although the heavy, twin-engined Bf110 had a poor record against British fighters its heavy armament meant that it proved to be deadly when attacking smaller bombers such as the Hampdens of No.50 Squadron.

festooned the air over the target. The raid was not a great success for the U-boat facilities were soon back in full working order.

On 1 October 1941 the squadron took part in an attack on Karlsruhe. Among the aircraft flying that night was the Hampden commanded by Squadron Leader R. Lloyd. The attack was made without incident, but as the aircraft returned over the Ardennes upper rear gunner and wireless operator Flight Sergeant Norman Bohn reported that a twin engined aircraft which he thought was a Junkers Ju88 nightfighter was following them. Lloyd banked his bomber to see if the other aircraft would follow, but at once the Junkers accelerated and opened fire. Both rear gunners fired back, and the Junkers was seen to catch fire and dive down steeply. A few seconds later an explosion was seen, and the night fighter was claimed as having been destroyed.

The attack had seen dozens of bullets lance through the aircraft and Lloyd was about to ask his navigator to do a quick inspection when a second shout from Bohn announced the arrival of a second night fighter, this time a Messerschmitt Bf109. This time Bohn did not hesitate, but opened fire at once. The German veered off and was seen no more. Lloyd now ordered the damage inspection to take place, but Bohn cut in to say that he had been wounded and was feeling faint. The lower rear gunner went to help and found that Bohn had been hit in the shoulder and that his flying jacket was soggy with blood. Bohn was dragged down to the fuselage floor where a first aid dressing was strapped on as he passed out.

Half an hour later the Hampden ran into thick cloud over the North Sea and Lloyd soon realised that he was lost. He asked the second gunner, and reserve wireless operator to call up the base in England and attempt to get a radio fix to establish a rough position for the aircraft. The man could not get the equipment to work and was wondering what to do next when he was amazed to be pushed gently aside by Bohn. His face deathly white and one arm dangling useless by his side, Bohn set to work. He too failed to get a response, and then passed out a second time. By sheer luck Lloyd managed to get back to find the Norfolk coast and put his bomber down at the first airfield he found. Bohn was carried out for hospital treatment. It was later found that the radio, although apparently intact, had been hit by a German bullet and was not working.

Flying with the squadron at this time was Sergeant Richard Trevor-Roper, who had joined in October 1940 and was still going strong. He began as rear gunner, but was promoted to wireless operator and it was in this capacity that he served for the rest of his time in the RAF, until killed in action in 1944. Trevor-Roper was considered to be able to work wonders with his equipment. Returning from one raid his Hampden ran into 60mph head winds and then a snowstorm. The radio control dials froze solid and it was only after much coaxing that he got the system to work. Obtaining direction fixes he found that they aircraft was almost 80 miles off course, but now they knew where they were they were able to get home safely.

One another occasion the Hampden was struck by lightning and the wireless transmitter destroyed, meaning that Trevor-Roper could only receive signals. Arriving over Britain at 11pm the crew found solid and very low cloud beneath them. They did not want to go down to land in case the cloud extended to the ground as fog, which would mean they would crash with fatal results. They were unable to ask for guidance as they could not transmit. The crew got ready to bale out, but with plenty of fuel on board the pilot, Wing Commander G. Walker, decided to give Trevor-Roper a chance to repair the radio. After an hour of frantic work while the Hampden circled over Lincolnshire Trover-Roper succeeded and made contact with the base at Oakington. Although cloud was at 200 feet, the Hampden got down safely.

Trevor-Roper later joined No.617 Squadron and flew with Guy Gibson on the Dambusters Raid. He was awarded the DFM during his time with No.50 Squadron, and the DFC with No.617, by which time he was a Flight Lieutenant. He was shot down and killed over Coburg by a Bf110 nightfighter on 31 March 1944 and lies buried in the Durnbach War Cemetery.

Sergeant Narin Robertson, who had been wounded flying with Sergeant Quinton, had returned to duty in September 1941 and was added to the crew of Pilot Officer Norman Goldsmith. On 27 December this crew was among those chosen to take part in Operation Archery, a commando raid on the Norwegian island of Vaagso.

The raiding force of 570 men was transported by the light cruiser HMS Kenya, with the destroyers HMS Onslow, Oribi, Offa and Chiddingfold, which provided gun support from offshore and had the task of sinking any German naval ships that sought to intervene. The main aim of the raid was to destroy fish-oil production and stores which the Germans used in the manufacture of high explosives. As a secondary aim, the raid had the testing of tactics and ideas for joint operations between the army, navy and RAF. Unknown to the British, the raid convinced Hitler that the British intended to invade Norway to cut off the German supply of iron ore. The Germans then moved more than 30,000 troops into Norway to guard against this non-existent threat.

The task of the RAF bombers was to destroy German gun emplacements and other positions on Vaagso at dawn, just as the commandos were going ashore. This necessitated a long flight out in darkness over the sea, with consequent navigational problems, followed by an equally long flight back in daylight when the Hampdens would be vulnerable to German fighters. In the event, the bombers found Vaagso without difficulty, bombing their targets accurately from a low height. Goldsmith went down to 150 feet on his

DUNKIRK BARGES, 1941
A photo issued to the press showing the barges berthed in Dunkirk that had been a target for a raid by No.50 Squadron in February 1941. The barges carried goods on the Rhine and their destruction would disrupt the German economy.

SCHARNHORST, 1942
No.50 Squadron were among the few to find and
attack the German battleship Scharnhorst when
that ship and its partner Gneisenau raced up the
English Channel under cover of bad weather in
February 1942.

bombing raid, allowing Robertson to spray bullets at other targets on the
island. However, the bomber was hit by return fire and the navigator badly
injured. Robertson negotiated the tricky interior passage of the Hampden to
reach the wounded man and administered first aid that, in the opinion of the
medical officer back at base, saved the man's life. In all 8 out of the 29 bombers
sent to Vaagso were lost, a heavy price.

On 12 February 1942 the squadron took part in one of the least glorious
events in the history of the RAF in World War II, though the fault was none
of No.50 Squadron's doing. The previous day the German battleships

Scharnhorst and Gneisenau and the heavy cruiser Prinz Eugen had left the French port of Brest under cover of low cloud. The ships had earlier been sent into the Atlantic to disrupt the convoy system and sink merchant ships bringing supplies to Britain. This time the local French dockworkers had been told the ships were heading for the South Atlantic and Indian Oceans, but in fact the Germans wanted to use them in northern Norway to block the Arctic convoys taking weapons to Russia. They intended the ships to steam straight up the English Channel to Germany, then move north after resupplying.

The German ships left Brest at 9pm, racing at top speed around Brittany and up the Channel. A British aircraft on routine patrol over Brest failed to spot the ships had gone. It was not until next morning that the British realised something was going on. An RAF radar operator in Dorset spotted unusual Luftwaffe activity with many fighters circling in mid Channel. These aircraft were, of course, escorting the ships. A pair of RAF Spitfires spotted the ships, but because they had no idea that the sighting was important they were slow in reporting them. It was not until noon, by which time the ships were steaming past Dover that the British responded. A desperate call went out from Bomber Command for any aircraft that could get into the air to do so and head for the Straits of Dover.

Among the 242 bombers that got airborne and headed south was the Hampden piloted by Goldsmith and with Robertson as the wireless operator. Only 39 bombers found the German ships in the dreadful weather that had closed in, and Goldsmith was among those. He at once went down low to drop his bombs, ignoring the heavy flak being thrown up by the German warships. One shell exploded just under the starboard wing, inflicting serious damage. Goldsmith had trouble holding the aircraft steady, so Robertson ripped the electric cord off his Aldis lamp and used that to lash the control column steady. The bomber limped to a nearby base and landed safely. With all the drama in the air, neither Robertson nor Goldsmith noticed if their bombs had hit the ships. In fact they had missed for no bombs hit the German ships, which suffered only slight damage from mines on their way to Germany.

The ability of three major German warships to steam with impunity up the Channel was a humiliation for the Royal Navy, and for the RAF. At least the men of No.50 Squadron had nothing to be ashamed of.

Into
Manchesters

In March 1942 the squadron was on the move again. This time they went north to RAF Skellingthorpe, a new base opened just west of the city of Lincoln. This base was altogether less comfortable than those that the squadron was used to. Accommodation, offices and messes all came in the shape of nissen huts that were often draughty, and reliably too cold in winter and too hot in summer. Barely had the squadron moved into its less than ideal new base than, in April 1942, the increasingly outdated Hampdens which still equipped No. 50 Squadron began to be replaced by an exciting new model of aircraft, the Avro Manchester. It was to prove to be an unhappy decision for No.50 Squadron.

On paper the Manchester was an effective and highly advanced design. Its overall performance was comparable to that of the Hampden with a top speed of 265mph, a ceiling of 19,000 feet and a range of 1,200 miles, but the airframe was quite different. It could carry 10,000lb of bombs, four times the load of the Hampden, and had a large bomb bay that was configured to carry a wide range of bomb types. The fuselage was wide, roomy and much more comfortable than that of the Hampden. The Manchester was much better defended as well. It had eight 0.303in machine guns mounted in powered turrets at the front, rear and on the back of the aircraft. In comparison the Hampden had only four machine guns, none of them in powered turrets. The bombaimer had a good position, hanging out of the front of the aircraft in a perspex bubble that gave him excellent all round views.

AVRO MANCHESTERS, 1942
An advert placed by Avro in a British newspaper in 1942 emphasises the size and bulk of the new type of bomber. The troublesome Vulture engine can be clearly seen, with its air intake

When the RAF began taking delivery of the Manchester from Avro, they were delighted with their new acquisition. Fast, heavily armed and able to carry a heavy bomb load, the Manchester promised to make the destruction of Germany's war industry a reality. But it was not long before crews began to report problems.

The most frequent problem was that one of the engines would suddenly break down half way to Germany. More alarmingly, several crews reported that an engine would suddenly burst into flames without any warning that something was wrong. The Manchester was equipped with the new Rolls-Royce Vulture engine. This powerplant was built on the new X-frame

A. V. ROE & CO. LIMITED AVRO Branch of Hawker Siddeley Aircraft Co. Ltd.

configuration and had 24 cylinders. It could deliver an awesome 1,780 horsepower and had been considered so important and effective that several airframes, not just the Manchester, had been designed around it by British aircraft manufacturers.

The problem was, however, that the sudden demand from the RAF for mass production meant that the engine was rushed into production before all the usual Rolls-Royce pre-production tests had been completed. Not until after the Vulture entered service were these checks completed and revealed problems with the lubrication system. Rolls Royce were confident that they could solve the problems, but the RAF was in no mood to wait. Instead it scrapped orders for Vulture-powered aircraft and reverted to designs powered by more reliable and proven engines.

MESSERSCHMITT BF109 REVVING, 1940
The Bf109 was Germany's standard fighter for the first two years of the war and proved to be a highly efficient destroyer of bombers. These are Bf109E models with square wingtips and a 20mm cannon in the nose.

The Avro company rose to the task. The fuselage of the Manchester was retained, given new wings and four Rolls Royce Merlin engines in place of two Vultures. The new design was to be called the Manchester MkII, but some wise head suggested that a completely new name was preferable so that crews were not prejudiced against the aircraft. So the Avro Lancaster was born.

While No.50 Squadron was flying Manchesters, the German air defences were becoming noticeably more effective. When the RAF night raids on Germany had started in earnest in 1940, the Germans had responded with what became known as the Kammhuber Line, named for the commander of Luftwaffe nightfighters who devised and introduced it. The Line consisted of an interlocking series of boxes measuring 32km by 20km that stretched from Denmark to central France. Each box had a central radar station that could pick up RAF bombers at night. Linked to the radar was a searchlight that could use the bearings picked up by the radar to find the bomber. Each box had a number of other searchlights operated by hand that used the more traditional technique of pointing the light at the sounds of engines to locate an aircraft. Each box then had either anti-aircraft guns or a prowling nightfighter that would seek to shoot down a bomber illuminated by searchlight.

When it was first introduced, the Kammhuber Line was equipped with relatively inaccurate Freya radars, and hampered further by the fact that the "nightfighters" were merely day fighter Messerschmitt Bf109 aircraft which lacked any specialist nocturnal equipment. Despite these handicaps, the Kammhuber Line took a toll on RAF night bombers. That toll mounted steadily as the German ground radar was improved, as was their system for calling up prowling fighters by radio to attack bombers.

By 1942, the Freya radar had been replaced by the more accurate Wurzburg system, while the nightfighters were equipped with early versions of the Lichentstein air-to-air radar. Together these two developments meant that a night fighter could be directed toward a bomber by the ground radar, then pick it up on its own radar with such accuracy that the German pilot could close in and open fire in total darkness. Very often the first a bomber crew knew of the presence of a German aircraft was a hail of lead. The British crews learned that they had to keep a sharp lookout in all directions from the moment they crossed the enemy coast until the moment they got back out to sea again on the return journey. The long hours of constant vigilance, knowing that at any moment deadly gunfire might erupt from the darkness proved to be terribly wearing on bomber crews.

Arriving at No.50 Squadron alongside the Manchester was a unique bomber crew that had already attracted a high degree of press interest. The crew was led by Flying Officer Harold "Mick" Martin and already had 13 combat missions to its credit. That was not unusual, what was unique was that this was the first bomber crew in the RAF that was composed exclusively of Australians. Many more Australians were serving in the RAF, but most were scattered among various squadrons and crews. Martin's crew had gathered a lot of press coverage Down Under, and came to No.50 with a fearsome reputation for low-level attacks and accurate bombing.

Retraining to fly the Manchester involved No.50 Squadron in a lot of work and reorganisation. For a start all the crews had to be reorganised. The Hampden had a crew of four, but the Manchester needed seven men. Once the new crews were formed, they had to fly a series of long and arduous training missions to get themselves accustomed to the new bomber and its handling characteristics. As one Manchester was setting off on one of these flights the Air Traffic Controller in the tower saw something a bit odd. He said nothing at the time, but later that evening in the Officers Mess he strolled over to accost Pilot Officer Richard Wiseman, the Australian pilot of the bomber concerned.

"Hi Dicky," said the controller. "Very funny thing today. I could have sworn I saw an ATS girl clambering into your Manchester."

"Oh yes, sir," replied Wiseman staring intently at a painting on the wall.

"Yes," came the reply. "Odd how your eyes can play tricks on you. Nobody would be fool enough as to take an ATS girl up for a spin." And he wandered off.

Wiseman breathed a sigh of relief. He had, in fact, been in the habit of taking up women from the local ATS (Auxiliary Territorial Service) unit at the request of the ATS staff. During his time with No.50 Squadron, Wiseman was awarded a DFC. When he got the bar to his DFC he was invited down to Buckingham Palace to receive the award from King George VI in person. Not having any family in the UK to take with him, Wiseman asked one of the ATS girls, a local Lincolnshire girl named Dorothy. They got on very well on the long train journey to London and back, began dating and by 1944 were married. She accompanied him back to Australia after the war.

Unknown to the men of No.50 Squadron, busy as they were coping with the new Manchesters, Bomber Harris and his staff had been working on a new and audacious plan that they code named Operation Millennium. Harris had only just taken over Bomber Command as a whole, and was under intense pressure at this time. The poor results achieved by Bomber Command to date had been largely due to the misconceptions about the type of war the RAF would be fighting that had dictated aircraft design in the pre war years. Those defects were now being rectified as the four engined Stirling, Lancaster and Halifax were starting to enter service, and greatly improved navigational

COLOGNE, 1942
The city of Cologne was the target for the first
1,000 bomber raid on the night of 30/31 May 1942.
The city centre was devastated and industrial
production fell. This photo was taken in 1945.

aids were not far behind. But bomber aircraft were expensive things to make and the crews were even more expensive to train. Both the army and the navy made continual demands for air support which were stripping resources away from Bomber Command. Harris remained convinced that by area bombing the industrial heart of Germany he could cripple weapons manufacturing and shorten the war. What he needed was an answer to his critics.

Harris therefore decided to mount one single, massive and hugely destructive raid on a German city. The raid would, he decided, be made by 1,000 aircraft in a single night. Not only that but a host of new tactics would be introduced to ensure accurate bombing and low casualties. The target would be marked by flares dropped by skilled navigators. The main bomber force would approach in a "stream", a mass of bombers flying close together on the same bearing and height, in the hope of swamping enemy defences. This opened up the risk of collision between bombers, so each aircraft was given a precise route to fly and times at which it was to be at different points.

A key problem that Harris faced was his lack of aircraft. Bomber Command had a force of about 400 front line aircraft ready for action at any given moment. That number could be boosted to around 600 by cancelling leave and holding back aircraft from routine patrols and other duties so that they would not be undergoing maintenance on the date chosen for the 1,000 Bomber Raid. Another 250 aircraft were promised by RAF Coastal Command, while other aircraft were scraped together from other sources. The target was fixed as Hamburg and the date set for full moon on 27 May 1942.

Then with just 36 hours to go the Royal Navy disrupted the plan by refusing to allow the Coastal Command aircraft to take part. Harris was unsurprised, knowing the navy wanted his bombers for itself. He therefore turned to newly trained crews who were undergoing operational conversion and asked them to take part. The response was enthusiastic and even crews not yet qualified volunteered to take part. Bad weather over Hamburg forced first a delay to 30 May, then a change of target to Cologne.

First into the air were aircraft from Fighter Command and Army Co-operation units. They flew over the North Sea to attack German night fighter bases and radar installations. As their attacks went in, some 40 bomber bases began throbbing to the sounds of heavy engines. In all 602 Wellingtons, 131 Halifaxes, 88 Stirlings, 79 Hampdens, 73 Lancasters, 46 Manchesters and 28 Whitleys lumbered into the air and headed for Cologne. Among the

AIRCREW ON AIRFIELD, 1941

Aircrew wander across a bomber airfield "somewhere in England" in 1941. Hangars, such as that in the background here, proved to be a tempting target for Luftwaffe raiders.

Manchesters were those of No.50 Squadron, taking to the air from RAF Skellingthorpe, near Lincoln.

Flying with No.50 Squadron that night was the crew led by Flying Officer Leslie Manser. The 20 year old Manser had been born in India, but the family returned to England when he was a boy. When he left Cox House School in

Hertfordshire in 1940 he volunteered for the army, but was turned down so he joined the RAF instead. He finished his basic pilot training in May 1941 and was sent to No.14 Operational Training Unit at Cottesmore for final training on Hampdens. He passed out on 27 August and was posted to No.50 Squadron, then at Swinderby. Two nights later he undertook the traditional baptism of fire for a bomber pilot when he flew as an extra second pilot with an experienced crew. The raid was to Frankfurt, and Manser did well enough to return to his own crew and be declared ready for combat.

Manser flew six missions in the following eight weeks. He impressed his seniors so much that he was considered good enough to be an instructor and was posted back to No. 14 OTU at Cottesmore. Manser was unhappy away from No.50 Squadron and made repeated requests to be sent back to his squadron. Instead he was sent north to Waddington to join No.420 Squadron, a new unit composed of Canadians, where he was again put to work as an instructor. It was not until April that he finally got back to No.50 Squadron.

Manser found the squadron in the process of converting to Manchesters, and on 8 April flew his first mission in a Manchester. It was a trip to Paris, where his load consisted of propaganda leaflets in French intended to harden the hearts of the French against the occupying Germans - pretty much a forlorn hope at that stage of the war. Manser and his crew took off five more times in the weeks that followed, but the Manchester proved troublesome and he had to turn back twice.

On 30 May the squadron was ordered to be ready to make a major effort. Everyone knew that Harris was planning something big, but nobody knew what it was. Manser was devastated to learn that the squadron had more crews than aircraft and that his crew had been chosen to stay behind. There was, however, a spare No.106 Squadron Manchester standing idle at RAF Coninghsby. Manser got permission to go and get it. The bomber was passed as airworthy and so, at the very last minute, Manser and his crew were fit to

---

COLOGNE CATHEDRAL
The twin spires of Cologne's medieval cathedral rise from the shattered ruins of the city centre in 1945.
No.50 Squadron bombed the city several times.
Cologne was Germany's fourth largest city and a major industrial centre.

LESLIE MANSER, 1942
Manser won a VC when flying with No.50 Squadron. He was one of the men who volunteered for the RAF after war broke out and completed his pilot's training nine months after joining.

take off in the Big Show. It was not until the briefing that the crews learned that they were going to Cologne, along with a thousand of their comrades.

That evening Manser's new aircraft, L7301 "D-Dog" was loaded up with more than a thousand 4lb incendiary bombs. It got into the air at 11.01pm and headed south along its specified course. Manser's height was set to be 18,000 feet, but at 7,000 feet the always difficult Vulture engines began to overheat. After a hurried discussion with his crew, Manser decided to press on at the reduced altitude rather than return to base. Other Manchester crews had done the same on earlier raids and reported that flak was less intense at lower altitudes as the German gunners concentrated on the main bomber stream above. But there was the risk that the aircraft might be hit by a bomb falling from above.

The rest of the flight out proved to be uneventful. But as Manser began his bombing run toward the flares and bomb blasts that marked central Cologne his Manchester was struck by a searchlight beam. The sudden, intense light temporarily blinded the crew, but Manser held the bomber steady and ordered bombaimer Richard Barnes to get ready. Caught in the searchlight, the bomber began to attract anti aircraft fire. The shells at first exploded a safe distance away, but as the seconds passed they crept closer and closer. After what seemed like an age, Barnes called out "bombs gone" and the Manchester gave the familiar spring upward as it was relieved of its heavy load. Manser pulled back on the control stick to begin evasive manoeuvres to get out of the searchlight beam. But it was too late.

A flak shell exploded directly under the Manchester, tearing off the bomb bay doors and sending razor sharp metal splinters lancing through the bomber. Manser pushed the nose down, twisting the heavy bomber into a diving turn that finally took it out of the deadly embrace of the searchlight. Manser called up his crew on the intercom then sent Wireless Operator Flying Officer Norman Horsley to inspect the damage to the bomb bay. He reported back that all the incendiaries were gone but that the racks were a mess.

Manser nursed the bomber back up to a height of 2,000 feet and turned for home. Only at this point did Naylor report that he had been wounded four times by shell splinters. Despite these injuries, Naylor had remained at his post, considering that until then the rest of the crew had their hands full. Horsley went crawling back through the fuselage to check on the wounded Naylor, helped him out of the turret and administered first aid. A few seconds later the port engine exploded and burst into flames. The fire raged along the port wing, threatening to set fire to the petrol tank that it contained.

VICTORIA CROSS MEDAL

The Victoria Cross (VC) is Britain's highest military award for valour in the face of the enemy. It was founded in 1856 and since then has taken precedence over all other orders, decorations and medals awarded in Britain.

Manser ordered co-pilot Sergeant Baveystock to feather the engine and operate the fire extinguisher. This had no noticeable effect, so Manser told him to try again. This time the flames flickered, then died.

The port engine was now useless and the bomber was losing height. Manser told his crew to throw out everything that they could prise loose. Item after item was heaved out of the door and flare shute, but the Manchester continued to lose height. Accepting the inevitable, Manser told his men to get into their parachutes and prepare to bale out. The starboard engine was now giving trouble. The bomber was losing both height and speed.

Front gunner Sergeant A. Mills had throughout this difficult time been scanning the dark skies for signs of German fighters. This was his first

COLOGNE ANGEL, 2006
Fixed to a pillar in Cologne Cathedral is this angel that serves as a memorial to the citizens of the city killed by Allied bombing. The cathedral was hit by bombs 70 times, but remained standing.

operational flight, the crew's usual front gunner being unavailable. What the novice Mills made of the mayhem around him can only be guessed at. When Manser gave the order to bale out, Mills was first out, dropping through the forward escape hatch. Horsley then dragged the wounded Naylor to the main door and pushed him out before jumping himself. Baveystock was about to jump when he realised that Manser had not yet got his own parachute on. Grabbing it from its rack, Baveystock began clipping it on to Manser's webbing harness. Manser pushed him roughly away.

"For God's sake, jump" shouted Manser.

The bomber gave a sickening lurch, hurling Baveystock down into the bombaimer's post. Looking down he saw the ground rushing past alarming close. With a final glance at Manser who was still in his seat wrestling desperately with the controls, Baveystock jumped down the hatch. He pulled the ripcord on his parachute, but he already knew he was too low for the parachute to open. He closed his eyes as the earth rushed up at him. Then cold blackness enveloped him. Realising that he was not dead, but was instead very wet, Baveystock kicked out and rose to the surface of what he soon realised was a drainage dyke. Baveystock looked round toward the sound of an engine to see the Manchester plunge into the ground and explode in flames. Manser had sacrificed his own chances of survival to save his crew.

Baveystock dragged himself from the waters that had saved his life. Remembering his training on how to act if shot down, Baveystock walked as far as he could that night, knowing the Germans would be searching the area around the crash for survivors. He then sought out a civilian, hoping that he was not in Germany. He wasn't, he was in Belgium. The man he accosted hurriedly gave him directions to a farmhouse where the farmer had contacts with the local resistance group. Within a few days Baveystock was in a safe house in Brussels where he met up with Horsley, Naylor and Mills. The rest of the crew had been captured by the Germans and spent the remainder of the war as Prisoners of War (PoW). The Belgian resistance smuggled the four men from Brussels to France, where they were passed from farm to farm on the long journey south to Spain, then over the Pyrenees and on to Gibraltar.

It was months before the crewmembers got back to England. When they did, they told of the exploits of their heroic captain. As a result Manser was awarded the Victoria Cross. The medal was presented to his family in March 1943. Forty years later, Manser's brother gave the medal to the RAF and asked them to look after it in perpetuity. It is now in the Imperial War Museum. When RAF Skellingthorpe was closed a school was built on part of the site. It is named the Leslie Manser Primary School. Baveystock was awarded a DFM for his leadership in getting the men home.

The great raid on Cologne during which Manser had died was judged to be a huge success. In all 868 bombers had found and bombed the target. Large areas of the city were laid waste, including 2,560 factories and workshops. About 45,000 people had been rendered homeless and another 150,000 fled the city to stay with relatives and friends elsewhere. The death toll on the ground had been 486, of which 411 were civilians, while the RAF had lost 43 bombers (3.9% of those taking part). The Germans later estimated that they had lost the equivalent of two months output from Cologne's factories. When reports from Cologne first started arriving in Berlin that night, they were not believed. The German high command simply did not believe that the RAF was able to mount such a large raid. When the Mayor of Cologne phoned Goering personally to try to convince the high command of what was happening, Goering told him he was "a stinking liar".

Not only was the damage heavy in itself, but it showed what Bomber Command could do to undermine German industrial output and was a huge morale boost to the British public.

Harris decided to launch two more "1,000 Bomber Raids" on Germany while his mighty force could be kept together. The first was sent to Essen in the Ruhr on 1 June. Bad weather intervened and the vast majority of the 956 bombers sent out got lost. Most managed to bomb something in the Ruhr, but few important targets were hit and the Germans did not even realise that a big raid was going on.

The third raid was on Bremen. This time cloud obscured the target, but flares marked the city accurately and most of the bombs fell on target. The damage was less than at Cologne, but still impressive. The Focke Wulf works were temporarily knocked out and the dockyards extensively damaged.

No.50 Squadron took part in all these raids. One of the men who flew on these raids, and who might have considered himself rather hard done by, was Sergeant Thomas Simpson, an Australian. After the raids he was recommended for a DFM not only for his "very high standard of gunnery and his efficiency" but also for his ability to calmly inform his pilot of the movements of German nightfighters, and so to allow the Lancaster to slip out of danger. For some reason that was never explained, the recommendation was not approved.

Simpson later flew as tail gunner in the crew of Mick Martin (another No.50 Squadron veteran) on the Dambusters Raid, and was awarded his DFM as a result. He survived the war to return to his native Australia.

The 1,000 bomber raids were not the end of the bombing effort sent out to Germany at this time. Although many bombers and crews had then to be withdrawn for maintenance, repair and other duties, others still flew to Germany. Among these was that of Flying Officer Southgate, with Sergeant Cliff Shirley as navigator. They were detailed to attack Bremen on 25 June as a follow up to the 1,000 bomber raid. Arriving over what Shirley declared to be the city, Southgate could see only solid cloud. Gingerly he put his bomber down through the cloud and emerged directly over the Focke Wulf works, which he promptly bombed.

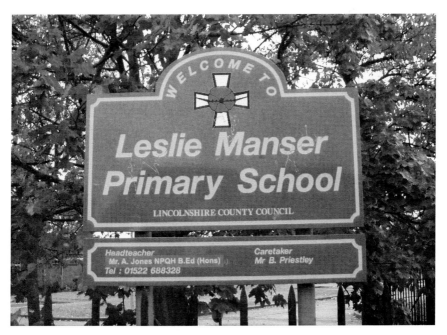

LESLIE MANSER SCHOOL
In 1981 RAF Skellingthorpe was closed and the land sold off for development. A school was built on part of the site and was named after Leslie Manser. (Photo: Claudia Aliffe).

The
Lancaster
Arrives

In May 1942 the first of the great, four-engined Avro Lancasters began to arrive at No.50 Squadron and within a month the last of the infamous Manchesters had gone. Although the Manchester and Lancaster were identical in many ways, the new bomber had Merlin engines in place of Vultures and proved to be popular with crews and effective in action.

The Lancaster also needed a longer runway than had the Manchester. RAF Skellingthorpe became a hive of activity as a swarm of workmen moved in

to extend the three runways. The work meant that the squadron was taken off operations for a while, and instead the men spent their time on training flights and brushing up on the academic side of their tasks. The local pub, acquired a new name - The Black Swan - as this was the radio call sign of the airfield.

Among the pilots who was delighted to ditch the Manchester for the Lancaster was Sergeant Paul Crampton. On one occasion he had had to fly all the way to Kassel and back at under 5,000 feet, and was down to only 300 feet by the time he got his Manchester home. At least the low height allowed his gunners to machine gun likely targets as they raced over Germany, with one power house blowing up with a satisfactory blast. Crampton and his crew had an even narrower escape on 1 August 1942 as they neared the end of their tour. They had just dropped their bombs on Dusseldorf when a flak shell exploded directly under the starboard wing. Both engines on that wing were knocked out, the radiator flaps jammed and the hydraulic system destroyed. On return to base Crampton weighed up his chances, then opted to perform that most dangerous of manoeuvres in a badly shot up bomber, a belly landing. Having alerted the base to have both fire engines and ambulances ready, Crampton eased the Lancaster gently down on to the turf beside the runway. In a torrent of screaming metal and flying clods of earth, the bomber got down safely, though the belly was ripped out and the aircraft had to be scrapped. Crampton and his crew successfully completed their tour in October 1942. One of his gunners, Sergeant John Kemp was given a DFM as the tour ended.

Flak could have a curious effect on men. Sergeant Gordon Cruickshanks was with the squadron at the same time as Crampton and completed his tour just a week later. Whenever flak bursts got close to his bomber, Cruickshanks would tell bad jokes to his comrades over the intercom.

Among the crews who converted successfully to the big four-engined

LANCASTERS ENTER SERVICE, 1942
The failure of the Vulture engine forced the Avro
Company to redesign the airframe of the
Manchester to take the more reliable Merlin engine,
and so produced the Lancaster bomber.

Lancaster was that led by Hugh Everitt, one of the oldest hands at No.50 Squadron. The Everitt crew included Robert Hay and gunner Donald MacDonald. Their first tour of operations was completed with No.50 in June 1941, by which time they had flown 30 missions and 192 hours of operations. They had one narrow brush with death in December 1940 when they ran into a sudden snowstorm over the Ardennes. The wings of the aircraft iced up, and an engine seized when its carburetter froze. Descending to a low altitude, Everitt admitted he was quite lost. MacDonald then succeeded in calling up base on the radio and despite the weakness of the signal managed to work out an accurate magnetic heading that allowed the navigator to plot a course home. MacDonald was awarded a DFM for his work on this first tour, while Everitt got a DFC.

On 8 June 1942 the crew returned to No.50 Squadron for their second tour of operations, this time on the Lancaster. This second tour passed without serious incident until 5 October when the crew were sent to bomb Aachen. This proved to be a difficult raid as bad weather closed in unexpectedly. Of the 257 aircraft sent out, only a third found Aachen at all. Among the bombers that got lost were the leading aircraft carrying the skilled navigators who were supposed to illuminate the target for others. Unfortuantely about 80 bombers pounded the Dutch town of Lutterade instead of Aachen, with consequent Dutch civilian deaths.

Everitt was one of these that did find Aachen. Over the target the aircraft was hit by flak. The fuselage was heavily hit and the fuel tank in the starboard wing had so many holes that the crew could see the streams of falling fuel sparkling in the light of the bomb blasts far below. So much fuel was being lost that it was clear that the bomber would never get back to base. Instead Everitt opted to head for an emergency landing field in southern England. Once again it was MacDonald who called up base to report the situation, get a bearing and arrange for the emergency services to be ready to receive the crippled bomber. And again he was awarded a DFM for his efforts. The bomber put down at West Malling in Kent, where it landed in a heavy crash landing and was written off.

The crew was given two days leave, and Everitt was desperate to visit his wife whom he had married three months earlier. She was living in Cardiff with his mother and it was thought quite impractical to travel all that way by train and back again in 48 hours. Fortunately one of the other crews at No.50 was due to take part in long distance navigational training and were successful

JUNKERS JU88, 1942
Although introduced as a bomber, the high speed
and long endurance of the Ju88 made it suitable as a
nightfighter. This captured aircraft bears an RAF
roundel was evaluated by RAF intelligence in 1944.

in registering a route to Cardiff and back again. Everitt clambered aboard as
a spare passenger and the Lancaster lumbered into the sky. As they were
approaching Cardiff, the pilot spotted a new and beautiful runway some
distance from his objective at St Athan Airfield. He landed, slowing just long
enough to allow Everitt to hop out, and then took off again for the return
flight to Lincolnshire. Everitt was at once confronted by a security guard who
announced that they were at Rhoose Airfield, and that it was not yet open.

"Well, it is open now," retorted Everitt before dashing off to hitch a lift into
Cardiff. Rhoose officially opened a few weeks later as a training base for
fighter pilots. It is now Cardiff Airport, the busiest in Wales.

The Everitt crew eventually finished their second tour without casualties
and were then taken off combat duties completely. Everitt himself rose to the
rank of Group Captain and by late 1944 was working in the Directorate of

Bomber Operations at the Air Ministry. While there he lived at home with his parents in Putney and so formed part of a curious link back to the very earliest days of No.50 Squadron. One evening Everitt and his mother were eating supper when they heard the familiar and dreaded noise of a V1 doodlebug heading towards them. Instantly the pair dived under the heavy dining room table as this was the only cover within sight.

"You know," mused Mrs Everitt as the deadly rattle of the V1 engine grew louder and louder, "I remember hiding under this table with you back in

1916 when you were still in nappies. It was the Zeppelins bombing us then, of course."

Meanwhile, the all-Australian crew of Mick Martin was continuing to impress. They were often tasked with flying in low to try to hit a specific, high value target within a city being bombed by the main bomber stream. At Mainz they went down to 5,500 feet to find and destroy their target. At Dusseldorf on 15 August they at first could not find their target, despite going down to 6,000 feet. The weather was terrible and after half an hour, the

LE CREUSOT, 1942
A photograph taken from one of the Lancasters on the famous Le Creusot Raid shows the bomber force flying low over a town in Vichy France on its way to the target. The daylight raid was deemed a success.

Lancaster was hit by flak and lost an engine. Martin turned for home having failed to find, never mind hit, his target. He was not alone. Of the 131 bombers on the raid less than half found Dusseldorf at all. Nobody on the ground was killed and the Germans lost no industrial output at all.

Two nights later Martin was part of a 139 bomber raid on Osnabruck. Again the weather was bad, but this time 111 bombers did find the right city and bombed the industrial area, destroying a paper mill, a copper wire factory, four military barracks and almost 100 houses. Martin was down low again, at 6,000 feet, and this time he successfully found and obliterated the military HQ that was his target.

On 24 August 226 bombers were sent to Frankfurt. This time Martin was given as his target not a structure in Frankfurt itself, but a building in Bad Kreuznach that lay under the route to be taken by the main bomber stream on its way to Frankfurt. The building in question was reported by intelligence to be the administrative headquarters of the German Western Army, which included the occupation forces in France and the Low Countries. Martin's bomber was given one of the new 4,000lb blast bombs that were then just entering service. So important was the target considered that the bombaimer Sergeant Henry Smith was given a special camera with which to photograph the results of their work. Martin detached his bomber from the main force on the approach to Bad Kreuznach, went down to under 5,000 feet and accurately bombed the target, which was obliterated. It was not his fault that the building turned out to be considerably less important than it had been thought to be.

"Mick" Martin was awarded the DFC during his time with No.50, but his greatest fame came in 1943 when he was on his second tour of duty. His reputation for low level flying and accurate bombing got Martin transferred into the newly formed No.617 Squadron formed especially for the famed Dambusters Raid of 17 May. Martin bombed his bouncing bomb accurately on the Mohne Dam before returning home. He later took part in numerous raids with No.617, on one of which he was shot down. Martin ended the war having flown on 49 bomber raids and 34 operations in Mosquito fighter-bombers. He remained in the RAF after the war, retiring in 1974 with the rank of Air Marshal.

By September 1942 the bomber crews and their commanders were well aware that problems with navigation meant that many crews were getting lost, or even worse thought they were bombing the right target when they had in fact bombed somewhere else. To gauge the scale of the problem bombers were being fitted with backwards facing cameras designed so that they would take a photo of the bombs bursting. The problem, so far as crews were concerned, was that this meant that they had to continue to fly straight and level after dropping their bombs for several seconds. In enemy skies alive with flak and nightfighters that could be highly dangerous.

On 19 September 1942, No.50 Squadron formed part of a force of 89 bombers going to Munich. It managed to produce photos taken by Flight Sergeant William Farrelly that triumphantly showed that part of central Munich had been obliterated, though most bombs fell among southern suburbs or in open country. Nine nights later Sergeant Colin Gray came back with equally impressive photos of a target in the Ruhr. Also in September Sergeant Fred Spafford came back with excellent photos of bombs hitting Saarbrucken as planned. These were rare flashes of light in the dark for far too often bomber crews at this point in the war risked their lives not knowing if they had managed to hurt the Reich much, or at all.

By October 1942 intelligence reports indicated that the vast Schneider Works at Le Creusot in central France had been converted by the Germans to make weapons. Harris was told that the works were to be his top priority target until they had been destroyed. A conventional Bomber Command night attack was ruled out by the fact that the works were surrounded by French civilian housing, and Churchill had ordered that casualties among the French were to be kept to a minimum during raids on France. After studying the problem closely, Harris decided that the best chance of success was to bomb in daylight. That would expose his crews to great danger from German fighters, so he timed the attack for dusk and ordered the bombers to fly out in a long route that took them down the Atlantic, out of sight of the coast of France, before cutting inland across territory held by Vichy France. The flight over France was to be carried out at or below 500 feet. Once the bombing had been completed, the bombers would climb to high altitude for a direct flight home under cover of darkness.

After a few days of intensive practice at low level flight, 94 Lancasters set out on the afternoon of 17 October. Among the No.50 Squadron crews was Sergeant William Batson who had begun his time with the squadron as a gunner before retraining as a bomb aimer. His task on this mission was to take photos of the works after the bombing. The raid went like clockwork, with the Lancasters encountering no German fighters on their way out. The greatest danger proved to be birds, which were hit several times by the low flying bombers. Batson was on one of the last bombers over the Schneider Works, taking photos that showed that heavy damage had been inflicted. Harris marked the target off.

Also on the Le Creusot Raid was a flight engineer by the name of Sergeant Albert Branch. He had earlier volunteered to fly with another crew on three missions to replace their regular flight engineer who was ill. Branch opted to remain with his regular crew to see them through their tour of 30 operations, and so was on his 33rd mission. When the crew landed safely back at base, Branch was writing up his log book when he realised that he was just 10 minutes short of 200 hours of operational flying.

BOMBAIMER, 1943
An RAF bombaimer peers from his prone position in the nose for a staged publicity shot. On daylight raids, such as that on Le Creusot, a bombaimer's job was even more crucial than it was usually.

The Le Creusot Raid came early in the career of Sergeant Victor Davis, one of the most talented Flight Engineers ever to serve with the squadron. His knowledge about the Lancaster was to become exceptional and highly respected. He was promoted to Flight Engineer Leader for the squadron when he eventually completed his tour of 30 missions with 203 hours of flying time in August 1943 he was awarded a DFM. Gaining his DFM rather earlier was Sergeant Peter Lynes, another Le Creusot veteran. He had joined the squadron on 22 September 1942, completing his tour of 31 missions on 26 April 1943. Even quicker to finish his tour was Le Creusot veteran the wireless operator Sergeant Ken Lyons, who joined the squadron in June 1942 and left in October 1942, again with a DFM.

Leading a flight of three Lancasters from No.50 Squadron on the raid was Acting Squadron Leader Philip Moore. He had already been awarded a DFC in August 1941 for general devotion to duty and courage in pressing home attacks in the face of enemy action. Now he was flying to Le Creusot, having already been on the great 1,000 bomber raids to Cologne and Bremen. He would go to Hamburg twice, Milan and Genoa. He was to get a bar to his DFC after Le Creusot.

Perhaps the best known crew of No.50 Squadron on the Le Creusot Raid was that led by Flight Lieutenant William Abercromby. Abercromby had joined the RAF as a ranker, being promoted to Sergeant in October 1940 and joining No.50 Squadron after he qualified as a pilot with the rank of Pilot Officer. By the time of the Le Creusot Raid he and his crew had already completed 26 raids. The crew were well known for their skill at low flying and for accurate bombing from rooftop height. Among the crew's feats already achieved was to score a direct hit with a high explosive bomb dropped from 5,000 feet on to a factory at Saarbrucken and to achieve an equally impressive hit on a target at Dusseldorf two nights later. On the latter occasion the bomber was coned by three searchlights as it left the target and was attacked by a Messerschmitt Bf109. Abercromby flung his heavy bomber around the sky almost as if it were a fighter, allowing his gunners to get a good shot at the fighter, which went down in flames.

Abercromby's next raid after Le Creusot was to be on the 28th to Milan. The raid was to end in tragedy. These raids on Italian cities were intended as much to undermine the Italian commitment to Hitler's cause as to degrade Italian industry. The need to avoid civilian casualties if possible was felt, so the raid took place in daylight and Abercromby went down to a height of just

100 feet to make sure he hit his target. Anti-aircraft fire opened up and although the aircraft was not seriously damaged, the rear gunner reported that he had been hit. Abercromby sent his mid upper gunner Sergeant Reginald Hutton back through the fuselage to drag the gunner from his turret and administer first aid. The wounds were clearly serious, so after patching them up as best he could, Hutton returned to his guns and hurriedly reported to Abercromby.

Abercromby decided that he had to put down as soon as possible, so wireless operator Sergeant Tom Burr was given the task of calling home base to arrange for the bomber to put down at a field in southern England and for an ambulance to be on hand. The radio failed to work, so Burr hurriedly went to work trying to repair the damage. After some improvised repairs the radio was made to work and a diversion arranged. Meanwhile, Hutton had returned to the wounded gunner and along with Sergeant Alan Connor, a cheerful Australian, rendered more permanent first aid, redressing the wounds with great care. Abercromby put his Lancaster down safely and the gunner was taken away, though he sadly died of his wounds some days later. Abercromby and the rest of his crew completed the rest of their tour without incident. The navigator Sergeant Alan Morris was awarded a DFM at the end of the tour, the citation stating that "he has, without difficulty, always led the aircraft to the target and through this quality the aircraft has been saved from passing over highly defended gun sites unnecessarily.

Abercromby went on to do a second tour with No.619 Squadron, where he earned a bar to his DFC in 1943.

One man on the Le Creusot Raid who turned out to have gained from the experience was Sergeant George Phillips. The usual wireless operater in the crew of Flying Officer James Cole was taken sick, so Phillips flew with Cole. The original wireless operator never returned to duty, so Phillips continued with Cole's crew. In April 1943 Cole finished his tour and was sent off to carry out test flights on a new model of Lancaster, the BII which had Bristol Hercules engines instead of Rolls Royce Merlins used on the BI. Phillips requested that he be allowed to take his entire crew with him for the new task, so Phillips was marked down as "tour expired" although he had flown only 24 missions. The BII did not prove successful since the Hercules engines consumed fuel more quickly than the Merlins, reducing the operational range of the bomber. Only 300 were built out of a total Lancaster production run of 7,400.

LANCASTER NIGHT BOMBER, 1943

By 1943 most RAF bombing was performed at night. As a consequence the undersides of bombers were painted black to hide them from anti-aircraft gunners and only the upper sides retained the familiar mottled camouflage.

Sergeant Richard Clarke also flew on the Le Creusot and Milan raids, as a flight engineer. The Milan Raid brought his number of missions up to 32, more than was required for a tour. He was then kept on at the squadron to train incoming flight engineers on the tricky business of keeping a Lancaster flying at optimal performance on long, lonely flights over the Reich, and when under fire. It was some time before the RAF noticed him and took him off the squadron for a rest. He objected strongly.

One No.50 crew that performed very well on the Le Creusot raid was that of the Australian pilot Les Knight. The crew had joined the squadron in September 1942 so they had flown nothing but Lancasters. By April 1943 the crew had completed 24 missions and 154 flying hours. Knight's wireless operator was awarded the DFM in that month, but then No.50 Squadron had to say goodbye to this popular crew. Their success at low flying had meant that they were picked out to join the special unit that was to become

No.617 Squadron, the Dambusters. Later low flying would be the undoing of Les Knight.

On a mission to bomb the Dortmund-Ems Canal on 16 September 1943 his Lancaster hit a tree, putting an engine out of action. Knight jettisoned his bomb and turned for home. Over Holland a second engine seized up. He got the heavy bomber high enough for his crew to bale out, but when he tried to follow them the bomber swerved violently to the left. Those on the ground watching saw the bomber dip toward the Dutch village of Den Ham, then lift again and turn aside as if the pilot were back at the controls and steering the bomber away from the houses and village school. Then the nose dipped again and the bomber ploughed into the ground. Knight was killed in the crash.

The rest of his crew survived, they had all been with him since No.50 Squadron days and had flown on the Dambusters Raid. Sergeant Raymond Grayston, Sergeant Frederick Sutherland and Sergeant Harry O'Brien were captured and spent the rest of the war as PoWs. Flying Officer Harold Hobday DFC evaded capture thanks to help from local Dutch farmers. He got back to the UK and returned to operational flying. He survived the war. Sergeant Robert Kellow DFM also evaded capture, but instead of returning to combat was posted back to Australia. Flying Officer Edward Johnson DFC similarly got back to Britain and flew no more missions.

A third No.50 crew that was taken to help from No.617 was that captained by Henry Maudsley. The crew flew on the Dambusters Raid, saw the Mohne Dam destroyed, and then flew on to attack the Eder Dam. Something went wrong with Maudsley's run and his bouncing bomb exploded on the surface of the water instead of deep below. His aircraft was badly damaged in the blast and crashed moments later. The entire crew of Henry Eric Maudsely DFC, John Marriott DFM, Robert Alexander Urquhart DFC, Michael John David Fuller, Alden Preston Cottam, William John Tytherleigh DFC and

---

LE CREUSOT AFTER RAID, 1943

A publicity shot issued after the raid highlights the heavy damage done to the main targets, though the undamaged areas lie just out of shot and go unmentioned. The man shown is raid leader Wing Commander Slee.

Norman Rupert Burrows were all killed instantly and now lie buried in Reichswald Forest War Cemetery.

On 9 November 1942 the squadron flew to raid Hamburg, part of a force 213 strong. Over the target there was heavy cloud and many bombers suffered from icing. The Lancaster flown by the New Zealander Flying Officer Ray Calvert was hit by flak. Calvert was wounded as was navigator Sergeant John Medani and the wireless operator was killed. The bomber lurched to one side and went into a diving turn that Calvert was only able to correct after much height had been lost. Calvert had a shell splinter embedded deep in his left arm, so he called the front gunner to render first aid while he continued to pilot the bomber. Medani, meanwhile, had administered his own form of crude first aid to the savage cut on his shoulder and continued to navigate the aircraft without complaining. The bomber was over the North Sea when Medani passed out from loss of blood, slumping over his table and smearing so much blood over the charts that nobody could make sense of them. Flying by dead reckoning, Calvert reached the coast of East Anglia and put the bomber down in a nasty crashlanding on a beach.

Also in November 1942 No.50 Squadron was joined by Wireless Operator Flight Sergeant Sam Allen. Allen's services were much in demand for his skills were undeniable. On a mission in a previous squadron his aircraft's electrics had failed and the bomber had become lost. Not wishing to risk running out of fuel over the North Sea by heading in the wrong direction, the captain of the aircraft had decided to get his crew to bale out, even though they would most likely be captured. Allen had asked for one last chance to find out where they were. Abandoning all hope of recognising ground features, he had managed to get a number of star fixes and by means of rapid calculations had found they were over Holland, not far from Rotterdam. The pilot had then set off over the North Sea and returned safely to base. But they had only just made it. There was less than 10 gallons of fuel in the tanks.

Amazingly, Allen was to repeat the feat almost exactly with No.50 Squadron. On 17 December 1942 his aircraft, piloted by Sergeant Geoffrey Harrison, joined a small raid of 18 aircraft on Soltau, a mining town in northern Saxony. The raid went well, but on the return journey Allen's Lancaster was hit by flak. One engine was knocked out, the elevators torn off, the hydraulics destroyed and much other damage done. As the aircraft gradually lost height over the North Sea, the pilot asked Allen to plot the quickest route to land. No bomber crew ever wanted to bale out over the sea as their chances of being rescued were slim. Once again getting out his star navigation equipment, Allen calmly took a series of fixes and then worked out a route that would get the crippled Lancaster to an emergency landing ground in the shortest time possible. Again, he got his crew home safely. Meanwhile, the bomber began to yaw to the left and it was only with the combined strength of pilot and flight engineer hanging on to the control stick that the aircraft was kept flying straight and level long enough to get back to Britain.

In the early months of 1943 the RAF introduced a new navigational system called OBOE. This system worked by bouncing radio signals from transmitters in England to a bomber over Germany and back again. The difference in time between the two returned signals could be used, through triangulation, to plot the position of the bomber. Although the bomber crew were not told directly of their position, the pulses in the OBOE signals were varied so as to instruct them to bear left or right as they flew toward their target. The system was astonishingly accurate, being able to get a bomber to within 100 yards of its target even when deep over Germany.

But OBOE had its problems. One was that its maximum range was about 250 miles. Another was that to work effectively the bomber had to fly on a straight course for some time, making it vulnerable to attack. In practice only the bombers that were to drop marker flares were equipped with OBOE. They dropped their flares, and the following bombers then bombed the flares.

It was not until mid-1943 that the Germans became aware of the system, and it took them some months to produce an effective countermeasure that jammed the signals sent from Britain. The RAF countered by varying the wavelength on which the signals were sent. There then followed a process of move and countermove that lasted to the end of the war. Generally the RAF stayed ahead of the game, but the Germans did achieve some notable successes in diverting or confusing bombers.

January 1943 saw the introduction of a second new navigational aid for RAF pathfinder bombers. H2S was a form of air-to-ground radar that enabled the operator in the bomber to "see" a map of the ground below him. The radar could differentiate between open fields, water, buildings and woods. Equipped with H2S and a good map, a navigator could find his way almost anywhere with a high degree of accuracy. Crucially it could work far beyond the range of OBOE and was thus invaluable on longer range raids, including attacks on Berlin.

The H2S had actually been produced many months earlier, but the RAF had hesitated to introduce it on operations because it used some new and highly secret technology. They feared that if a bomber carrying H2S were to be shot down the Germans would get hold of the hardware and use it to upgrade their own defences. The dispute over whether or not to introduce H2S raged for months. Harris wanted to use it, the scientists disagreed. In the end Churchill himself intervened, sending a peremptory note to the head scientist ordering him to release H2S to Bomber Command at once. Complications over the manufacturing technique meant that H2S was slow to enter service in numbers, but by July 1943 it was in regular use among pathfinders.

At first ordinary bomber crews had to cope without such sophisticated help as H2S, but as the months passed more and more bombers were equipped with H2S until it was standard issue for bombers operating at night over the Reich.

Some bombers had narrow escapes. On 20 April 1943, during their 26th mission, the crew piloted by Sergeant Francis Huntley were sent to bomb Stettin (now Szczecin in Poland) as part of a 339 strong force. The target was beyond OBOE range and much faith was placed in the ability of the lead aircraft, now known as Pathfinders, to mark accurately. Huntley was flying at only 900 feet in the hopes of avoiding the attentions of the German defenders, but the ruse had not worked. Over Denmark he was set upon by three Ju88 nightfighters. Huntley skilfully weaved the heavy bomber around the sky, doing his best both to spoil the aim of the Germans and to ensure that his own gunners could get the attackers in their sights. The first German overshot, the second stayed warily out of range while the third pushed home its attack, but was then shot down in flames by fire from Sergeant Alan Stott in the tail turret on the Lancaster. The attack had, however, disabled the rear turret, shot away the starboard elevators and damaged the rear part of the fuselage. After a discussion with his crew, Huntley abandoned the mission, dumping his bombs into the sea and heading for home. It was not until they got back to Skellingthrope that the crew realised that the flaps and trimming tabs had also been damaged. That made landing a tricky exercise, requiring the efforts of pilot and flight engineer at the controls, and even then the heavy bomber almost ran into the perimeter fence before it came to a halt.

Even luckier was the crew of Sergeant John McCrossman which on 29 May 1943 set off to bomb Wuppertal as their ninth mission over Germany.

On its run into Wuppertal the Lancaster was hit by flak which knocked out one engine completely and seriously reduced the power output of a second. The bombing run was completed, and McCrossman turned for home. It was soon apparent, however, that the aircraft was losing height. McCrossman ordered his crew to start throwing overboard anything that could be disengaged. A second flak shell then struck, damaging the hydraulics and causing the bomb bay doors to flop open. The increased drag caused the

BOMBER HARRIS AT DESK, 1943
In February 1942 Sir Arthur "Bomber" Harris took over as Commander in Chief of Bomber Command. He introduced rigorous new training methods and insisted on novel tactics in the air.

aircraft to lose height more rapidly and by the time the Lancaster crossed the Dutch coast they were down to just 500 feet.

By this point the crew were hurriedly unscrewing and unbolting anything that was not welded in place and throwing it overboard. Even the doors went. Flight engineer Sergeant John Wilkinson was meanwhile glued to his controls trying to keep the remaining engines going. By the time the Lancaster limped over the English coast it had gained a little height, so McCrossman opted to fly on to Skellingthorpe rather than put down at an emergency landing ground. He got home later than any other pilot, but with all his crew uninjured. "This behaviour", noted the station commander, "is characteristic of Sergeant McCrossman."

The Wuppertal Raid was to become famous as the first time that an entirely new phenomenon took place, though at the time it was not recognised for what it was. The raid was concentrated at the key industrial area known as Barmen, where factories, workshops and houses were jammed tightly together. The bombers dropped a mix of high explosive and incendiary bombs, the idea being that the blast bombs would damage buildings. The following incendiaries would then set fire to exposed roof timbers and so destroy by fire buildings that had only been damaged by the explosives.

Barmen had never been bombed before and its emergency services were inexperienced in dealing with the effects of bombing. Moreover those men who had shown promise had been moved to cities that were more regularaly bombed. To make the situation doubly worse, the chiefs of the fire service, police service and air raid service had all gone away for the weekend. The bombing by the 719 bombers was very accurate due to good marking by the Pathfinders and ideal weather conditions. The heavy damage proved to be quite beyond the inexperienced and leaderless emergency services in the town. The fires took hold as expected, then spread rapidly among the tightly packed buildings to create a single enormous blaze. The heat generated by the great fire created a large column of rising air that sucked in fresh, cooler air from outside the town. This in turn fanned the flames and fed them with fresh oxygen, increasing the intensity of the fire and accelerating the column of rising hot air, thus repeating the process. In all 1,000 acres, around 75% of Barmen's built-up area, was destroyed by fire along with five of the town's six largest factories, 211 other industrial premises and nearly 4,000 houses.

On the night of 20 June 1943 No.50 Squadron was over Friedrichshafen on the shores of Lake Constance near the Swiss border. The target of this raid was very specific, the factory where were made the Wurzburg radar sets that were crucial to German air defences. The raid introduced two novel techniques. The first was that a single and highly exprienced bomber pilot was over the target to take control of events. He supervised the marking by the Pathfinders, kept in radio contact with the bomber crews and monitored the activities of the German defences. This role would later be formalised as the Master Bomber. The second innovation was that the raiders did not return to Britain but instead flew on to land in North Africa, thus evading the nightfighters prowling the skies to the north. Only some 10% of bombs hit the factory, but that was enough to disrupt production for some weeks and most of the other bombs hit nearby industrial estates.

The Lancaster in which Flight Sergeant Leonard Cook was bombaimer had just started its run into Friedrichshafen when the tail gunner reported that they were being stalked by a nightfighter. Seconds later the mid upper gunner spotted a second German aircraft, and then a third. It was highly unusual for three nightfighters to be so close together, but Cook remained calm and kept calling out the instructions to keep the bomber on target. It was just after the bombs had been dropped that the three fighters attacked, and the bomber corkscrewed away from danger.

On the return from the raid on Friedrichshafen Sergeant Albert Cooper finished his tour of operation, having completed 33 operations and 188 flying hours. He was a popular member of the squadron and everyone agreed that he deserved some sort of recognition for his calm bravery in the air and cheeful boisterousness on the ground. The problem was that he had not done anything outstanding, nor had his aircraft been involved in anything dramatic. Almost in despair the senior officer wrote about him "Although there is nothing outstanding to show, his cheerful manner and willingness to fly make him worthy of consideration for the award of the Distinguished Flying Medal." Perhaps surprisingly, the medal was awarded.

A week later on 28 June the squadron went to Cologne as part of a force of 608 bombers that had railways works as the main target. Over the city one of the Lancasters had a flak shell burst immediately under its nose. The perspex cupola through which the bombaimer worked and the navigator peered was ripped off and the resulting rush of air into the nose of the bomber blew all but one of the navigation charts out. Navigator Sergeant John Heath was, moreover, hit in the shoulder by shrapnel. This was, however, Heath's 23rd mission and he was unfazed by his sudden problems. Propping himself against the side of the damaged bomber he managed to navigate the bomber back over Germany, Holland and the North Sea to return to Lincolnshire. It was only after the bomber had landed that he informed the pilot that he had been wounded and would rather appreciate an ambulance.

Another Lancaster of the squadron had an equally adventurous time over Cologne that night. Flight Sergeant Morral Cole had just piloted his bomber over the aiming flares when the Lancaster gave a sudden lurch. Cole struggled to get control of his bomber, fearing it had been hit by flak. Calling up his crew over the intercom for reports, Cole learned from his tail gunner, Sergeant Frank Pointon, that the bomber had been hit by incendiary bombs dropped by another Lancaster higher up. Pointon reported that none of the incendiaries had ignited, and all had fallen off the bomber. However, said Pointon, his own turret was now non operational. Cole piloted the bomber away from Cologne, north to the North Sea and then headed for base. It was only once they were out over the sea that Pointon informed Cole that he had been wounded and was now feeling woozy, probably from loss of blood. The

LANCASTER CREW AFTER MILAN RAID, 1943
The north Italian city of Milan was one of the most important industrial cities in Italy and so came in for some of the heaviest bombing directed at Mussolini's war effort by the RAF.

mid upper gunner was despatched to give first aid, and was astonished to find that Pointon had had the index finger sliced clean off his left hand.

A few days later one of the squadron's longest serving crews was stood down having completed their first tour of operations. The crew led by Flight Lieutenant Philip Stone had joined the squadron in the summer of 1942 and had by this date completed 34 missions and 201 hours. Stone was awarded the DFC for the tour, and his Wireless Operation Sergeant James Moore was given the DFM. Gunner Sergeant Donald Penfold was also awarded a DFM and was then sent off to train as an air gunnery instructor so as to pass his skills on to the next generation of men going off to bomb the Reich.

A constant worry for bomber crews was the long sea crossing to and from their targets. On the return journey many crews in damaged bombers had to decide whether to risk the sea crossing or to bale out over enemy occupied Europe. Not only did the sea offer little chance of survival if they were forced to bale out, but even if they managed to crash land their bomber and scramble into a life raft, the chances of being picked up were unpredictable. More than one bomber crew died a lingering death in their life raft due to thirst and exposure. It was not a nice way to go.

On 8 July on their way back from Cologne one Lancaster was hit by flak just as it crossed the coast. The attack knocked out three engines and caused extensive damage to the wings. As the pilot struggled to keep the bomber level, wireless operator Flight Sergeant John Short calmly established radio communication with the Royal Navy air-sea rescue service and gave the bomber's position. Seconds later the pilot shouted out to brace for a crash landing into the sea. As the heavy bomber smacked down on the sea, one of the wings erupted into flames as the ruptured fuel tank caught fire, the flames spreading rapidly toward the fuselage.

The inflatable dinghy was hurriedly thrown out and the crew raced to get in it and paddle it away from the flaming wreckage. It was with huge relief that the crew saw about an hour later a fast naval patrol boat approaching, brought to them by the location broadcast by Short.

On 30 July Flight Sergeant Morral Cole was piloting a bomber, one of 273 sent to attack the previously unbombed Remscheid in the Ruhr. By this date Cole had been given a new tail gunner to replace the injured Pointon. After dropping its bombs the Lancaster was caught by a searchlight and soon two others had got the bomber coned. Cole hurled the heavy bomber into the tricky manoeuvre known as the corkscrew. This involved putting the aircraft into a diving turn to port until it had lost 1,000 feet of height, then continuing in a climb to port for 500 feet at which point the rudders were put hard over so the aircraft began to climb to starboard. After gaining a further 500 feet of altitude, the pilot put the nose down for a turn to starboard, losing 500 feet before putting the rudder back over into a diving turn to port. The pilot then had to get back on the level while his crew scanned the air around them for signs of the enemy.

Cole successfully threw off the searchlights, but was then coned again and was forced to corkscrew a second time. Again he escaped the lights, but a night fighter must have located him for seconds later the bomber shook as it was hit by a torrent of cannon shells. The rear gunner was killed instantly, the tail smashed to pieces, the elevators torn off, the hydraulics damaged, causing the undercarriage to come down, and the fuel tanks in the starboard wing badly ruptured so that fuel poured out over the wing. The bomber went out of control and turned over on to its back as the starboard outer engine caught fire. Cole wrestled with the controls while his crew tried to get back on their feet and the flight engineer shut down the burning engine and operated the extinguisher.

After some tense minutes, Cole got the Lancaster back on an even keel and gave the order to bale out. The crew, however, held a hurried conversation and decided that they did not want to bale out over Germany where they would certainly be taken prisoner. They asked Cole if he thought he could get the bomber to occupied Holland, where they would at least stand a chance of getting in touch with the resistance. Cole agree, but had to get his front gunner to help him hold the control stick steady as it was constantly pulling to port and threatening to put the bomber into a spin.

By the time the bomber had got to Holland, however, things had quietened down considerably. The three remaining engines were running well and fuel loss had stopped. Cole suggested that they try to get back to England. Despite the likelihood of a watery grave if the bomber went down over the sea, the crew agreed. Tense minutes later the bomber limped over the Kent coast and put down at the first airfield it reached. The survivors were safe. It had been only the crew's eighth mission.

It was in the summer of 1943 the crews of No.50 Squadron, along with the rest of RAF Bomber Command, began to be painfully aware that a new and potent German weapon had entered the fray. The standard German attack tactic was to stalk the bomber from the rear. This allowed the German both

FOCKE WULF FW190

The FW190 is widely credited as being the most effective German fighter of the war. Although other fighters were technically better the FW190 was reliable and produced in large numbers.

to confirm that the target was a British bomber, and gave him the opportunity to gauge its speed and course in order to open fire with accuracy. The problem, from the German point of view, was that the bomber offered a fairly small target from the rear, while the rear turret was equipped with four machine guns able to fire back with accuracy and effect.

Some Luftwaffe nightfighter pilots began to attack from below. After stalking the bomber they would dive to about 1,500 feet below the target, then climb almost vertically to get within firing distance just as their own aircraft began to stall. This allowed them to rake the bomber with bullets and cannon shells while having a larger target to aim at and less danger of return fire. There were, however, some casualties among Germans who overshot and rammed the bomber, while others were destroyed when their fire set off the bomb load.

In 1943 the Luftwaffe began installing a system termed Schragmusik ("weird music"). This consisted of a pair of cannon mounted vertically in the nightfighter behind the pilot. The German then had simply to position his own aircraft underneath a targetted bomber and open fire to send a stream of cannon shells upward into the hapless British bomber. So effective was this development, that the Germans began arming most of their nightfighters with the weapon, introducing a horribly effective 50mm cannon version to be fitted into their own bombers, now converted for night fighting duties.

No.50 Squadron first encountered Schragmusik on the night of 17 August 1943 when it took part in one of the most important and secretive raids of the war. That afternoon when the crews were called to their usual pre-mission briefing, the senior officer present made it abundantly clear to them that their mission that night was of the highest importance. He told them that the reasons for the destruction of the specific target were so top secret that he could not tell them for the simple reason that even he did not know. But he did tell them that orders from the very highest level of government had come that the target had to be destroyed. He then read out a written order direct from Bomber Harris himself. "If the attack fails, it will be repeated the next night and on ensuing nights regardless of casualties until the target is destroyed." A stunned silence followed this chilling announcement.

After that dramatic and startling opening, the briefing continued. The target was not to be any large industrial city, nor any target anyone in the room had ever even heard of – it was to be a small island just off the German Baltic coast, east of Denmark.

What nobody in the briefing room knew was that the island of Peenemunde was being used by the Germans for the development of new and terrifyingly effective secret air weapons. These would eventually see service as the V1 and V2, weapons which laid waste areas of London and other places in southeastern England during 1944. Once they realised just what the Germans were making at Peenemunde the British government had become very worried. Not only were pilotless flying bombs and ballistic missiles new weapons of unknown but probably terrible effectiveness, but they had the potential to damage greatly civilian morale. Churchill himself had ordered the bombing raid on Peenemunde.

The operational orders for the Peenemunde raid turned out to be as unusual as the start of the briefing. That night there was to be a full moon, and the weather over the target was predicted to be cloudless, clear and bright. Bombing was to be carried out from a height of 7,000 feet, less than half the usual bombing altitude for Lancasters, and bomb aimers were warned that the target was so small that every bomb had to land within 300 yards of its aiming point.

The bomb aimers were warned that it was expected that as soon as the raid began the Germans would set up a dense smoke screen over the target. No.50 Squadron, coming in towards the end of the raid, would therefore use a new method dubbed "time and distance" that they had been practising for some weeks. This involved using H2S radar to identify a key ground feature - in this case the mainland coast - and then flying straight and level at a set speed for a designated amount of time on a pre-determined course that should see them directly over the target. The bombs would then be released even if the target could not be seen.

It was not just No.50 Squadron that was being sent on this highly unusual raid. In all 324 Lancasters, 218 Halifaxes and 54 Stirlings were going to bomb the island. In addition 28 Mosquitoes were being sent to Berlin to drop flares as if they were marking the Reich capital for a major bombing raid. It was hoped that this would lure most of the German nightfighters to Berlin, leaving the route to Peenemunde clear. In case that did not work bombing raids were to be carried out on nightfighter bases across northern Germany earlier in the evening of the raid.

Again a Master Bomber was to be in command on the spot, circling high overhead throughout the raid and giving radio orders to the main bomber force as the raid took place. On this occassion the Master Bomber noticed that some of the marker flares were incorrectly placed, and ordered new flares to be dropped before the first wave of the bomber stream arrived at 00.15am. The first wave attacked the living quarters of the scientists and technical experts - the only example throughout the war when Bomber Command made inflicting casualties, as opposed to material damage to buildings and transport links - the primary objective of a raid. The second wave hit the industrial workshops at 00.30am.

Then it was the third wave, including No.50 Squadron. They attacked the experimental station further north, but due to problems with the novel time and distance technique most bombs missed. Even worse some 25% of the force were late in arriving and did not clear Peenemunde until almost 1am. By that time the German nightfighters that had been lured to Berlin were racing back to attack what the Germans now knew was the main bomber force out that night.

STATUE OF HARRIS

The statue of Bomber Harris that stands outside the
RAF church of St Clement Danes in central
London. It was erected in 1992, some eight years of
Harris's death at the age of 91.

Most of the nightfighters were FW190 single seat fighters, but two were Messerschmitt Bf110 two seater fighters with schragmusik. Those two twin engined fighters shot down six bombers in the minutes that followed, while the FW190s accounted for another 29 bombers. Another six British aircraft were lost to anti-aircraft fire.

The total of aircraft lost would have been higher by one had it not been for the exceptional night vision of Flight Sergeant Sydney Proctor. In the days before infra red night goggles, the ability to see well in the dark was highly prized among Bomber Command crews. The gunners had to scan the black skies constantly for signs of a shape slightly blacker than the already black background. Such a dark smudge would be the first sign of an approaching nightfighter. Proctor was gifted with fine night vision and on many previous occasions had spotted a nightfighter early enough for him to alert his pilot and for the Lancaster to dive away from danger.

This night he spotted a prowling FW190 when it was till some distance away. But when the Lancaster took evasive action, the German followed. Clearly the German had night vision every bit as good as Proctor's. The FW190 accelerated to the attack. Proctor waited until the German was well within range before opening up with a destructively accurate burst of fire from his four machine guns. The FW190 shuddered as the bullets hit it, then the engine burst into flames and it spiralled earthwards to destruction. The Lancaster flew on home unscathed.

Another narrow escape was enjoyed by the crew of Flight Sergeant Joseph Thompson. The tail of this bomber was hit by incendiaries dropped by another bomber that smashed one of the tail planes and jammed both rudders. Despite this damage, Thompson managed to get his bomber home safely.

Bombing the Reich

Although No.50 Squadron had long since discarded their Hampdens, they remained engaged in "gardening", the dropping of mines off the German coast. On 19 September they were asked to drop such mines to block the entrance to the naval harbour of Gdynia in occupied Poland. Chosen for the task was Joseph Thompson and his crew. They were already known for their ability to make precision raids at low level. Going down exceptionally low, Thompson dropped his mines just a few hundred yards from the harbour entrance, bottling up two German cruisers for several days until minesweepers had gone out to clear the mines.

In October 1943, No.50 squadron acquired a new pilot who had already enjoyed a rather unusual RAF career, and whose future life was to remain curiously entwined with No.50 Squadron for the next forty years. Michael Beetham was born in London in 1923 and went to Marylebone Grammar School. As a schoolboy he watched the Battle of Britain raging overhead, and endured the bombing of the Blitz. As soon as he was old enough he volunteered for the RAF and was assigned to ground crew. After a year on the ground he volunteered for pilot's training and was sent to the USA for

LANCASTER SQUADRON TAKING OFF, 1943
By 1943 , No.50 Squadron was one of two dozen RAF squadrons flying the Lancaster, while many others flew Halifaxes or Stirlings. These big, four-engined bombers were at least inflicting serious damage on Germany.

MICHAEL BEETHAM, 1943
Photographed during his time
with No.50 Squadron, Beetham
was a mere Flying Officer when
he bombed Berlin ten times in
1943. He later gained the
exalted rank of Marshal of the
Royal Air Force.

instruction. He qualified as a Flying Officer in June 1943 and after his time at OTU learning to fly a Lancaster he was posted to No.50 Squadron.

Beetham arrived with No.50 Squadron just in time to join the Battle of Berlin, and he flew to bomb the Reich capital no less than 10 times in the weeks that followed. The Battle of Berlin in which No.50 Squadron played such a role was begun by Harris with the intention of bringing home to the capital of the Third Reich the brutal realities of war. For years the German people had been living high off the plundered resources of conquered territories. Soldiers had been stealing fine clothes, jewellery and other personal items whenever they could and sending them back to the folks at home. Productive farmland had been systematically stripped of crops to ensure high standards of food in German shops, while the conquered farmers had to eke out an existence on starvation rations. Through all these years Berlin had largely escaped heavy bombing. The city was simply too far from Britain and too heavily defended to be a worthwhile target. But with large numbers of heavy four-engined bombers, effective navigation and a growing ability to counter German defences, Harris decided it was time that Berlin was hit, and hit hard.

Between November 1943 and March 1944, Berlin was subjected to 16 massive attacks by up to 800 bombers, and there were dozens of smaller raids during this time. About 4,000 Germans were killed and up to half a million made homeless. Vast industrial areas were laid waste and the transport network seriously disrupted. The cost to the RAF was heavy with 1,047 bombers lost and 1,700 damaged. In all 2,700 crewmen were killed and over 1,000 captured. The concentrated attacks on Berlin ceased in March 1944 partly because the shorter nights made raids deep into the Reich more difficult and partly because Bomber Command was being called upon to attack targets in France in preparation for the D-Day landings.

On 28 January 1944, Beetham and his crew were on a mission to Berlin as part of a well concentrated and highly effective attack on the southern industrial suburbs of the city. Beetham was making his final run in on the target with front-gunner Flight Sergeant Albert Bartlett peering through the bombsight when the tail gunner shouted a warning that a German night fighter was stalking them. The enemy was a Junkers Ju88, almost certainly equipped with schragmusik. Despite the danger, Beetham continued on the run and released his bombs. The German then made his attack, with Beetham managing to veer off course just enough to spoil his aim. Bartlett, meanwhile, had scrambled back into the front turret and hurriedly opened fire. Chunks flew off the wing of the Ju88, which then dived away out of sight and did not return to the attack.

Also flying with the squadron in the Battle of Berlin was Sergeant Charles Brown, a rear gunner. He flew to Berlin five times, Hamburg twice and the Ruhr six times as well as other targets. On three different occasions his bomber was attacked from the rear by a German night fighter. During one such attack, over Berlin no less, Brown poured an accurate burst of machine gun fire into the twin engined German and saw an engine emit sparks as if it were about to catch fire. Unlike others in similar circumstances, Brown did not make a claim and it was not until his pilot claimed a "damaged" on his behalf that Brown got any credit.

Bizarrely there was a second rear gunner named Brown, this time Sergeant Hamilton Brown, with the squadron at the same time. He too was credited with a "damaged" German night fighter in February 1944 and opened fire on enemy aircraft on five other occasions during 19 flights to Germany during that long, bitter winter.

The hat trick of air gunners named Brown flying with No.50 Squadron over the winter of 1943-44 was completed by Flight Sergeant Sidney Brown, a mid upper gunner. He went to Berlin six times, Hanover three times,

Hamburg, Nuremburg and Manheim twice and to other targets. On 21 October his bomber was attacking Leipzig and had just released its bombs when the rear gunner called that a Ju88 was attacking from behind. Brown sighted the German illuminated by the flashes of exploding bombs below and opened fire at the same time as the rear gunner. The concentrated fire of six machine guns proved too much for the German, which veered off with an engine on fire and then went into a vertical dive toward the maelstrom below. Both Brown and the rear gunner believed the nightfighter to have been out of control. When they landed they claimed it as destroyed, but were much annoyed when the intelligence downgraded their claim to probably destroyed as they had not actually seen it crash or explode.

The squadron did not go only to Berlin at this time. In December 1943 they flew to bomb Leipzig, which had then recently been promoted to being a priority target after military intelligence learned that the Germans had moved ball bearing manufacturing to the city. Nobody in the RAF knew which factory was being used for ball bearings, so the entire industrial area was designated the priority target.

When still more than 50 miles from Leipzig the Lancaster piloted by Flying Officer James Lees was struck by a hail of bullets from beneath, presumably from a nightfighter equipped with schragmusik, though nobody on the bomber saw their assailant. One bullet missed Lees by inches, going on to smash the windscreen in front of his face. He was at once hit by a blast of intensely cold air as the sub-zero air over Germany in mid-winter howled through the gap in the perspex to strike him flat in the face. Other bullets pierced the fuselage in numerous places, but the only serious damage done was to immobilise the rear turret. Unfortunately the turret jammed in such a position that the gunner could not get out. The only exit for the gunner would come after the bomber landed and ground crew could smash their way in to him - assuming the Lancaster got that far.

Lees went on to bomb Leipzig, but on his way back to England the hydraulic system failed completely. Mindful of the plight of his tail gunner, Lees flew on to reach his home base and executed what the official record terms "a masterly landing", though in fact it left his bomber a wreck. But the tail gunner walked free untouched.

Another bomber hit by a night fighter on its way to a target was that of Flying Officer Russel Lloyd, whose Lancaster was peppered by bullets as he approached Berlin for the tenth time. This time it was the mid upper turret

PILOTS SHOWN TARGET, 1943

By 1943 bombers were increasingly asked to aim their bombs at coloured flares dropped by target markers who had arrived early in the raid. Pilots were still tasked with getting their aircraft over the correct target on time.

that was knocked out of action, and again the hydraulics were knocked out. Lloyd too went on to bomb his target and returned home.

Pilot Officer Douglas Toovey never found out what it was that damaged his engine on his way to bomb Magdeburg in January 1944, but one of his starboard engines suddenly burst into flames. The extinguisher was activated and the flames went out but the engine was useless. Toovey bombed the marked target successfully, but on the return journey the Lancaster began slowly but inexorably to lose height. Over the Netherlands the bomber was hit by flak and the port flaps destroyed. Nevertheless Toovey struggled on to Skellingthorpe where he completed a perfect landing.

That aircrew did not always correctly identify what they saw on missions was shown on one mission over Berlin when the Lancaster in which Flight Sergeant Joseph Rodgers was tail gunner was attacked by a night fighter. This was Rodgers's seventh nocturnal combat with fighters, so he should have known what he was about. His skill at shooting could not be denied for as the fighter swept past the Lancaster he and the mid upper gunner both poured bullets into their opponent, which then caught fire and dived vertically to destruction. When the crew returned to base, Rodgers identified the fighter as having been a Messerschmitt Me210 twin-engined heavy fighter.

The Me210 had entered service in late 1941, intended to replace the Bf110. It was armed with two forward firing 20mm cannon alongside two 7.9mm machine guns, plus two further 13mm machine guns mounted in remote controlled barbettes on the side of the fuselage. The Me210 had a top

LANCASTER BOMBS DUISBURG, 1944
This Lancaster is dropping an 8,000lb "cookie", a blast bomb designed to shatter buildings, and a cluster of incendiaries intended to set fire to wooden beams exposed by the "cookie" – a lethal combination.

speed of 350mph and a ceiling of 23,000 feet. On paper it was an awesome weapon of war, but the reality was very different. The aircraft was very difficult to fly and prone to nosedive into the ground on take off with fatal results for the crew. The Luftwaffe was understandably unimpressed and cancelled its order for 1,000 Me210s after just 90 had been delivered. By the time Rodgers reported his Me210, the fighter was no longer being used as a nightfighter over Germany. He must have seen a Bf110, or perhaps an Me410 instead. Such errors were fully understandable in the stress of combat, and the extent of such misidentifications has never been clear.

One eventful sortie to Berlin in February was undertaken by the crew of Flight Lieutenant Thomas Blackham. Over western Germany the bomber was subjected to anti aircraft fire that came without searchlights, and was presumably aimed by radar. One shell damaged the elevators, but the bomber was otherwise untouched. A few minutes later a nightfighter that nobody on the Lancaster ever saw opened fire and bullets riddled the rear part of the bomber. The rear turret was put out of action, though the gunner was uninjured, and numerous holes punched through the fuselage. Though nobody on board at the time realised it, the oxygen equipment had also been damaged. Believing the damage to be slight, Blackham chose to push on to Berlin.

As Blackham began his bombing run he began to feel light-headed and called up the rear gunner to see how he was, but there was no answer. Two other members of the crew also failed to respond to Blackham's increasingly worried calls. The bombaimer, however, continued to give the calm directions necessary, so Blackham pushed on to drop his bombs. Once the deadly load had gone he asked the flight engineer to investigate and the damage to the oxygen was discovered. The flight engineer effected a hurried repair and soon the unconscious crew members were awake once more. The return trip was uneventful and three nights later the crew went out again, this time to Augsburg.

In the midst of the Battle of Berlin, Beetham and his crew were on a training flight over Lincolnshire when one of their engines caught fire. The flames spread rapidly and the on-board extinguishers had no effect. Beetham ordered his crew to bale out, holding the aircraft steady while they did so. Then he too jumped and all came down safely. Beetham did not only fly to Berlin, but also on other raids during this long winter. Over Augsburg he lost an engine, but managed to get his aircraft home against the odds. He was awarded the DFC after that raid, though his citation makes no mention of the reasons for the award.

On 30 March 1944 Beetham and the rest of No.50 Squadron took off to form part of a raid of 795 bombers sent to pound Nuremberg. The target area was to be the part of the city where aircraft factories were located. The weather forecast was for cloud for most of the route out and back, but clear skies over Nuremberg.

The raid was a disaster. The cloud cover proved to be absent, and the Germans introduced a new tactic called "tame sows". This involved heavily armed twin-engined night fighters being directed by radar to join the stream of bombers. They then mingled with the British aircraft before opening fire from within the British formation. The tame sows not only shot down 85 bombers - the heaviest RAF loss of any raid of the war - but they so disrupted the bomber stream that bombing was erratic and damage on the ground minimal. Beetham was lucky, bringing his Lancaster back unscathed.

On 6 June 1944 British, Canadian and American troops stormed ashore in Normandy in the D-Day landings. The landings transformed the war in the west, drawing ever larger numbers of German troops, aircraft and tanks into battle in France and draining reserves away from the armies fighting the Russians. It also led to a number of changes for Bomber Command as they were asked to attack targets in France to assist the Allied armies, as well as attacking more strategic industrial and transportation targets in Germany.

On 15 June, the Lancaster in which Flight Sergeant Dennis Pierson was tail gunner bombed vast fuel and ammunition stores at Châtellerault in France. On the way back it was attacked by a Junker Ju88 nightfighter over northern France. Pierson watched the German aircraft manoeuvring prior to launching its attack and kept up a running commentary over the intercom to his own pilot. When the German accelerated to begin its attack, Pierson began the usual tail gunner's task of judging when to open fire. If he opened fire too early his bullets would spread out ineffectively, but the muzzle flashes from his guns would give the German an ideal aiming point. If he left it too late he might be killed by the German's bullets before he got off a single shot himself. Judging the moment right, Pierson opened fire and then got the shock of his life. The Ju88 exploded in a gigantic ball of fire and flame that illuminated the night sky for miles around, dazzled Pierson and sent a flash of heat burning through the perspex of his turret. The comment uttered over the intercom by the mid upper gunner was unprintable.

AVRO LANCASTER FRONT TURRET
The front gunner of a Lancaster was equipped with twin 0.303in machine guns mounted in a powered turret that could turn through a wide arc of fire. His feet rested in stirrups that dangled over the bombaimer.

This was not the only time that Pierson was to be surprised by the effect of his guns. A few weeks later his bomber was high over Germany when he again saw a German nightfighter stalking them. Again he began the nerve-shredding business of calculating when to open fire. This time when he pressed the firing button nothing happened. His guns were jammed by ice. Fortunately the German missed the Lancaster, which flew on home unscathed.

By this stage in the war, dropping bombs was not the only task given to bomber crews over the Reich. As if they did not have enough to do, they were also given a number of other jobs to carry out. Flight Sergeant Alfred

Spruce, for instance, was reckoned to be one of the better wireless operators in the squadron. He was therefore given the task of transmitting back to base meteorological information such as cloud cover, wind direction, wind speed and air pressure. Once an hour he had to take these readings and transmit them back to base. That he managed to carry out this onerous task whenever asked to do so was noted with approval and played a part in gaining him a DFM when he finished his tour of operations in March 1944.

Danger did not only come from German night fighters. On 20 April 1944, just as the squadron was getting airborne to bomb railway yards at La Chapelle, the inner starboard engine on one of the Lancasters suddenly shut down. The bomber gave a lurch, and the pilot had to react quickly to stop a crash. Flight Engineer Sergeant Albert Darby, meanwhile, quickly found the problem and got the engine restarted. He was reporting his actions on the intercom when the starboard outer engine then cut out and the bomber again dipped down to the ground that was still only a couple of hundred feet below the bomber. Darby got the new engine going again, but recommended that the mission be aborted.

Darby's skill was called on again on 7 July when his bomber was attacked by a nightfighter over the V1 storage depot at St Leu d'Esserent. A fire broke out on the starboard wing and despite everything Darby could do it continued to flicker away as the nightfighter made repeated attacks. As the gunners drove off their assailant, Darby carried out a stringent check of his equipment and again tracked down the problem. He assured the pilot that the fire was not dangerous and would not affect the performance of the engines. On Darby's assurances the pilot opted to fly home rather than bale out. They got home safely.

By this date the squadron was commanded by Wing Commander Anthony Heward. In April he was awarded a DFC, the citation reading "Wing Commander Heward has devoted much of his skill and energy in training of other members of the squadron with excellent results. His leadership has inspired all." Heward went on to command No.97 Squadron in 1945, where he was awarded a bar to his DFC, and later held a string of senior staff appointments. He ended as an Air Chief Marshal in 1974 and retired in 1976 having also become a Knight Commander of the Bath.

Rather less exalted in rank, but no less courageous was Flight Sergeant Frank Knott who completed his tour of 33 missions and 185 flying hours in July 1944. Knott was a tail gunner who had had what must have been a terrifying introduction to air combat. On his very first mission, to Nuremberg, his bomber had been attacked by a German night fighter from the rear as it began its bombing run. Knott shot back, but neither he nor the German seemed to hit anything. Minutes later the fighter was back, making a second, third and fourth attack. As the bomber left the target area a second night fighter pounced, diving down out of the darkness to pepper the fuselage of the Lancaster with bullet holes. Again, Knott shot back, this time the mid upper gunner added his fire to the stream of bullets lancing out from the bomber. This time definite strikes were seen on the German aircraft, which flipped over and dived away to be seen no more. Over the Netherlands, yet another nightfighter found Knott's bomber and attacked. It came back again and again, but again neither the German nor Knott scored any obvious hits. In all the Lancaster was attacked ten times that night. They were lucky to get home in one piece.

On the night of 6 July toward the end of his tour, Knott's Lancaster was again attacked by a German nightfighter - this stime identified as a Bf109. On its first pass the German scored several hits on the starboard wing of the bomber, rupturing the fuel tank and setting fire to the escaping fuel. Knott shot back with determination, and a good aim. The German had pieces shot away from its wing, going into a steep dive and disappearing from sight. Knott claimed it as "damaged"

Victory over Berlin

B y 1944 it had become accepted that bomber crews had to complete a Tour of Operations that was composed of 30 missions before being taken off operational duty. There had been complaints that some crews were sent to long distance and more dangerous targets, such as Berlin, while others were tasked with hitting comparatively easy targets in occupied France. There therefore developed a system by which a raid to Germany was counted as a full mission, while those to France were counted as fractions of a mission depending on the target. In 1943, when German defences were at their most effective, a crew's chances of surviving a full tour was about 50:50. By 1944 the odds of survival were rather better, and they continued to improve as the war neared its end.

One man serving with No.50 Squadron who completed his tour at this time was Flight Sergeant Norman Bacon. He had flown to Berlin ten times, Frankfurt three times, Stuttgart twice and had also bombed Munich, Nuremberg, Leipzig, Kassel, Essen, Schweinfurt and a host of other targets. Throughout this time, Bacon had not done any single feat of outstanding bravery, but his consistent cheerfulness and devotion to duty were outstanding and were reckoned to have played a large role in keeping up morale in the squadron. He was therefore recommended for, and awarded, a DFM.

Going one better was Flight Sergeant William Beesley who, on 8 August 1944, completed his second Tour. These second tours were of 20 missions and after a second tour had been completed the crewman was stood down from operational flying permanently. Beesley had completed his first tour with a different squadron, but in his time with No.50 had attacked Berlin twice, Schweinfurt, Magdeburg, Stettin and Frankfurt, as well as numerous other targets.

While it was usual for crews to stay together throughout their tour, there were always occasions when illness or wounds meant that a man could not fly. Every squadron had on its books men who could plug these gaps and who flew with a wide variety of crews during the course of their tour of 30

LANCASTERS BOMB IN DAYLIGHT, 1945

By 1945 the air defences of the German Reich had become so weakened that No.50 Squadron and other bombers of the RAF could at last bomb in daylight as a matter of course.

missions. One of the strangest such men to serve with No.50 was Flight Sergeant Fred Burton, who completed his tour in August 1944 and was awarded a DFM for his trouble.

Burton was a highly skilled navigator whose services were much in demand, and all crews who temporarily lacked a navigator were happy to have him on board. What made Burton unusual is that he always developed the most blinding headaches when taken to altitudes above 15,000 feet. He had managed to cover up this problem during his training, but it emerged during his time with No.50 Squadron. The medical officer tried to get him to give up flying, but Burton refused point black declaring that he had joined

THE REICHSTAG, 1945
The massive damage inflicted on the German capital by the RAF and USAAF was largely done in the last year of the war by which time there were a large force of bombers able to reach the city.

the RAF to fly, and fly he was jolly well going to do. It was largely because of this grim determination that he was put forward for the DFM.

It was unusual for men to complete their second tour of operations for the simple reason that the odds of their surviving 50 missions over the Reich were less than 50:50. Still more unusual was it for a man to volunteer for a third tour of operations. One such man was Bernhorst Botha, a South African who led a remarkable career. His family were Boers who had fought against the British in the Boer Wars. When World War II broke out the Bothas backed Germany and young Bernhorst was urged to volunteer for the Luftwaffe. After some discussion he opted for the RAF instead and took ship to Britain.

Botha did his first tour as a sergeant gunner in 1942. In 1943 he retrained as a pilot and completed his second tour as a Pilot Officer. He was then promoted to Flying Officer and came to No.50 Squadron for his third tour. On 27 June 1944 he was awarded the DFC for his "outstanding keenness and his determination to press home his attacks". During his time with No.50 Squadron, Botha got into several scrapes. He once borrowed – without asking permission – the station commander's car for a run into Lincoln for an evening with his crew. On the way back the rather inebriated Botha put the car into a ditch. He was charged by both the police and the RAF, but escaped with a fine.

Another time he was out on a navigational training mission when he got bored with the stooging about while the trainee navigator on board was put through his paces. Seeing ahead of him a line of electricity pylons, Botha put down the nose of the Lancaster and thundered under the high tension wires with only feet to spare. He was reported by a local civilian and again ended up on a charge.

On one of his last missions, to Aachen, Botha saw one of his engines seize up soon after leaving Skellingthorpe. Standard procedure was to turn back if an engine failed soon after take off, but Botha decided to carry on regardless. Over Aachen the Lancaster was hit by flak and a second engine ceased working, then fell off completely. Now down to only two engines Botha headed for home. He managed to land safely at Skellingthorpe, but the bump of landing shook loose a propeller which flew off and cartwheeled away over the airfield leaving his bomber with only one working engine. Another charge followed for endangering his aircraft and crew.

Botha's final brush with authority came when a visiting wing commander spotted that his Lancaster sported the painting of a naked and very attractive blonde on its nose. The senior officer ordered it removed immediately. Botha retaliated by painting a highly unflattering caricature of the wing commander on his aircraft instead. By this point Botha's time at Skellingthorpe was almost up, so the station commander merely rolled his eyes and had the new decoration painted over.

Botha completed his third tour in the autumn of 1944 and was awarded the coveted Distinguished Service Order (DSO), the citation for which read "Flight Lieutenant Botha has a notable record of operations. He has completed a very large number of sorties, both as an air gunner and pilot, against many heavily defended targets in Germany. He has at all times displayed great determination and courage in pressing home his attacks and has undoubtedly assisted in maintaining the high standard of morale in his squadron." When the war ended Botha was awarded the American DFC to add to his British DFC and DSO. He survived the war to die peacefully in 1991.

In August 1944 the squadron was sent to attack the great U-boat base at La Pellice in southwestern France. The raid was led by a relative newcomer to the squadron, Squadron Leader Dennis Stubbs. Stubbs had volunteered for the RAFVR in March 1939, as did so many other young men when war seemed close. He qualified as a fighter pilot with the rank of sergeant in July 1940, but after a minor accident was not allowed to fly until August. He then joined No.601 Squadron and fought throughout the rest of the Battle of Britain. Early in 1941 he had been transferred to train as a pilot instructor and was then moved to South Africa to train young men entering the RAF to be fighter pilots. Late in 1943 he volunteered to retrain as a bomber pilot and early in 1944 joined No.9 Squadron. He moved to No.50 in June and was given command of B flight. On 24 July he flew to Stuttgart, but the weather proved so bad that for five hours he could hardly see out of the windows and flew on instruments alone.

The La Pallice raid was to prove highly controversial among the high command, and very tricky for the men sent to carry it out. La Pallice was the fourth of the great U-boat bases established by the Germans in occupied France, the others being Brest, Lorient and St Nazaire. At intervals throughout the war Bomber Command had been asked by the Navy to attack these bases. The targets had always been difficult, and not only because they were heavily defended. All four bases were built inside French ports, which themselves lay within large French towns with thousands of French civilian residents. Every time the navy asked the RAF to bomb them, the government had stepped in to insist that French casualties be kept to a minimum. The resulting arguments had usually meant that the U-boat bases were not attacked. Only a very few, low-level raids by picked crews had taken place.

The only time that this pattern had varied had been in January 1943. At this date the losses of merchant ships to U-boats was at its height and the navy was more insistent than ever that the bases had to be bombed. At the same time intelligence reports and RAF reconnaissance flights showed that the Germans were constructing massive concrete structures over the U-boat pens. These structures were so massive that it was estimated that no bomb then in existence would so much as dent them. If the U-boat bases were not bombed soon, there would be no point in bombing them at all. The decision to ignore the likelihood of French civilian casualties may have been influenced by the fact that many of those civilians were working in the docks.

As a result, Harris was ordered to attack. He started at Lorient and in the course of three raids badly damaged the U-boat base, and destroyed 75% of all buildings in the town. St Nazaire was next, but while the town was virtually ruined the U-boat base remained operational. Bomber Command was then ordered to cease attacking the French towns. Instead the USAAF, which by early 1943 was operational in fairly large numbers, was asked to undertake a series of precision daylight raids. These caused minor disruptions to the U-boat operations, but soon the vast concrete structures were complete, hiding within them all the repair and maintenance facilities the U-boats needed. The USAAF too called off its attacks.

The decision for Bomber Command to have another go at La Pallice in August 1944 was, therefore, unexpected. The decision had been prompted by intelligence reports that the German war effort was becoming critically short of fuel oil. La Pallice was chosen because the oil works serving the U-boat pens stood on the coast away from the town and could be easily identified due to the unique configuration of the coast and a nearby island. The pens themselves were to be attacked again, this time with newly developed 2,000lb amour piercing bombs that, it was hoped, would be able to crack open the concrete roofs of the pens.

The first attack was scheduled for 9 August, but low cloud meant that the attackers could see little. They dropped their bombs, but could not see the results. The following day they went back and this time were more successful. The oil works were bombed accurately and successfully. The U-boat pens were hit repeatedly with the new bombs, but even these novel weapons proved to be useless against such vast masses of reinforced concrete. The U-boat pens are still there.

One innovation on these two raids came in the shape of half a dozen long-range Mosquito fighters provided by No.100 Group. These were sent to provide at least some fighter escort to the bombers, though on neither of these raids were German fighters encountered. The presence of nightfighter escort for the bombers would become increasingly common over the winter of 1944-45, and Luftwaffe nightfighter attacks would become less of a threat accordingly.

Stubbs's leadership of the La Pallice raids was considered to have been exemplary, and he was awarded a DFC. In November 1944 Stubbs was to leave No.50 to become a Pathfinder, and then a Master Bomber. At the end of the war he was awarded the DSO and opted to remain in the RAF. He rose steadily through the ranks to reach the position of Group Captain. He died suddenly in 1973 at the age of 55.

August 1944 also saw the squadron's first encounter with a deadly new German fighter: the Messerschmitt Me410 "Hornet". This aircraft had been developed as a fighter-bomber and ground attack aircraft, but a nightfighter version was soon produced and began entering service in numbers in April 1944. This formidable aircraft had two 20mm cannon and two 7.9mm machine guns in the nose operated by the pilot, plus two 13mm machine guns and a 50mm cannon in side and ventral mounted barbettes controlled remotely by the observer from his seat behind the pilot. With a speed of 317mph and ceiling of 32,000 feet the Me410 could outperform the Lancaster with ease, while its heavy armament ensured that it was easily able to shoot down any bombers that it encountered.

Despite the awesome reputation that the Me410 quickly established, No.50 Squadron came off best in its first encounter. It was tail gunner Flight Sergeant Hywell Lewis who spotted the German coming up behind his Lancaster. Calmly and clearly he described the German's movements to the pilot, who responded equally calmly with a description of what manoeuvres he was about to do. When the German made its attack, the Lancaster sideslipped out of the way to give Lewis a clear shot at the German. He poured 400 rounds into the Me410, which caught fire and flashed past the bomber. The German seemed to go out of control and dived, still burning, vertically down to pass through a layer of cloud and be lost to sight.

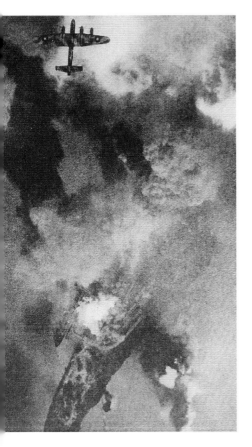

LANCASTER HITS OIL DEPOT, 1945
Seen from a higher-lying bomber, a Lancaster clears its target of burning oil storage works. Oil had been a key target for the RAF throughout the war but had not always been able to find, identify and destroy the targets until daylight raids were possible.

The encounter with the Me410 came just a few weeks after Lewis, jointly with nose gunner Sergeant Ernie Manning, had shot down a Bf109 in daylight. By this stage of the war, Bomber Command had returned to making daylight raids on lightly defended targets close to Britain. On 25 July the target was St Cyr. The Bf109 attacked in clear light, but again it was Lewis's description of its bearings and manoeuvres that meant the Lancaster's nose gunner could get effective bursts in. Front gunner Manning was having a busy time for he was not only the gunner, but also the bombaimer. Having poured 150 rounds in the German and having had the satisfaction of watching it crash into the ground, Manning scrambled down into the perspex nose dome and just five minutes later dropped the bombs accurately on to the target. Two minutes later he was back in his gun turret scanning the skies for the German fighters. His pilot was so impressed that he recommended Manning for a DFM, which was awarded when the crew finished its tour in September having flown for 183 hours on 34 missions.

Some events in the air could not be explained. On 18 September 1944 the squadron was flying as part of a force of 206 Lancasters to bomb Bremerhaven on the north German coast. The target had not been bombed before as it was a relatively small port, and its position made it difficult to find. On the way to the target air bomber Flight Sergeant George Richards felt his bomber start to wobble in flight, then its nose went down and the Lancaster entered a dive with its engines running at full speed. Richards scrambled out of his compartment to find the pilot slumped unconscious over the controls. Working with the flight engineer, Richards wrestled the dead weight of the

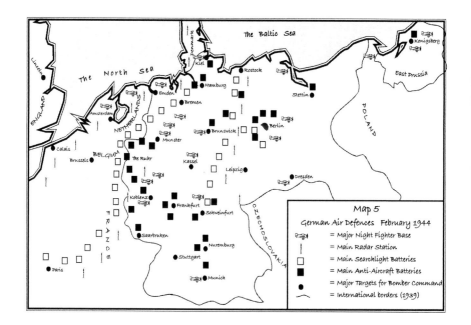

GERMAN AIR DEFENCES, 1944
In the first months of 1944 the Reich's air defences were at their peak with an integrated system of radar, anti-aircraft guns and night fighter bases. The system inflicted a heavy toll on No.50 Squadron.

pilot out of his seat. Richards then took his place and grabbed the controls to pull the heavy bomber out of its dive when it was barely a thousand feet about the ground.

Richards jettisoned the bombs and stretching his flying skills to the limit turned the heavy bomber for home. The flight engineer searched the pilot for signs of a wound, but could find nothing to explain his sudden lack of consciousness. Richards had meanwhile got the bomber up to a safe height, but was getting nervous about having to land the heavy bomber back at base. The pilot slowly came out of his faint a couple of hours after collapsing and by the time the bomber was back at Skellingthorpe was well enough to land. The pilot subsequently went to see the medical officer, but nothing was ever found wrong with him and he never again suffered such a fainting fit.

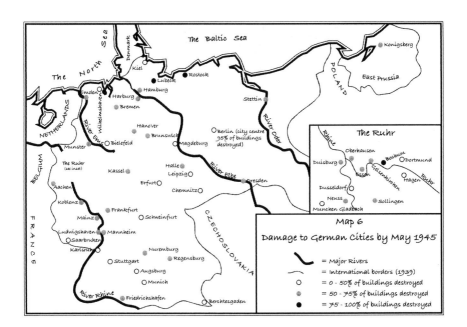

DAMAGE TO GERMAN CITIES, 1945
The physical damage inflicted on German cities by the RAF was awesome. Some cities were almost totally destroyed and others had their centres obliterated. By 1945 Germany was prostrate.

On a mission over Bremen on 6 October 1944, the Lancaster piloted by Flying Officer Ronald Amey was hit by a flak shell that exploded inside the bomb bay seconds after the bombs had been dropped. The blast not only caused severe damage, but also began a number of fires inside the bomber. Amey guessed that his aircraft was doomed and used the intercom to order his crew to bale out. He then undid his harness and climbed out of his seat, only to be confronted by the grim sight of his navigator unconscious, covered in blood and lying on top of a burning parachute. Quickly grabbing the intercom, Amey countermanded his order summoned help to the navigator and grabbed the controls to regain control of the bomber. A searchlight then came unnervingly close to the Lancaster, so Amey threw the bomber into evasive manoeuvres.

Wireless Operator Sergeant George Lane was, meanwhile, trying to put out the fires with the on board extinguishers. The violent movements of the bomber caused him to drop one extinguisher and spoiled his aim with the second. Having run out of extinguishers, Lane then grabbed the navigator's bag and began beating out the flames. When the bag caught fire, Lane threw it out the cockpit window and went back to work with his gloves. Those too caught fire, inflicting nasty burns on Lane's left hand, and were thrown out. Lane then remembered the thermos flasks of hot tea stashed beside the pilot's seat. Grabbing those he emptied the tea on to the last of the fires and managed to put it out.

Amey then ordered the gunner who had been caring for the navigator to return to his turret, and it was Lane who now cared for the wounded man. Having checked the dressings and administered morphine to the poor man, Lane returned to his wireless and after much effort managed to get a homing signal by means of which Amey was able to navigate back to England. Although the bomber had sustained much damage, Amey managed to put it down at the emergency landing field perfectly and medical men swarmed aboard to care for the badly wounded navigator. Only then did Lane mention his burnt hand and was himself whisked off to hospital.

Lane was recommended for the Conspicuous Gallantry Medal, next down from the Victoria Cross. In the event, however, he was awarded the DFM.

This raid of Bremen makes for a clear indication of how destructive Bomber Command had become by this date. The port and industrial city of Bremen had been attacked 31 times since 1939. The effectiveness of the attacks had varied depending on the weather and the skill of the crews, but whatever damage was inflicted had proved to be only temporary. Within weeks the port had been working again and little disruption had been caused to the Focke Wulf aircraft works. This raid by 246 Lancasters utterly destroyed the port, destroyed the transport infrastructure and demolished the FW works. Bremen was never attacked again, for there was nothing left worth bombing.

On 1 February 1945, No.50 Squadron was sent to take part in a raid on Siegen, a metalworking centre in Westphalia. The raid by 271 Lancasters proved to be ineffective as strong winds blew the marker flares off into open countryside, which was then pounded by the bombs. Sergeant John Bridger was upper mid gunner on a Lancaster which had a quite uneventful flight to the target. Bridger was, as ever, peering into the darkness for signs of any German nightfighters prowling around the bomber stream. Looking up he saw the ominous shape of an aircraft directly above, then he realised that it was another Lancaster. Bridger called a warning over the intercom just as his own aircraft dropped its bombs on target. At once the bomber shook violently and several large holes appeared in the wings and fuselage as the bomber above them dropped its load of incendiaries. Most of the small bombs crashed straight through Bridger's aircraft, but one crashed straight into his gun turret, smashing the perspex dome and flinging Bridger from his perch.

Bridger found himself dangling upside down, caught in the leads and wires that festooned his seat. His right leg was numb and paralysed, but even worse he saw just ten feet away an incendiary rolling around the floor of the fuselage suddenly splutter into life and begin to burn. Calling for assistance, Bridger struggled free and grabbed a fire extinguisher to tackle the deadly incendiary. The rear gun turret had jammed, and the gunner inside was trapped with a second incendiary igniting against the door between the turret and fuselage. The first bomb put out, Bridger ran down the fuselage and kicked the incendiary away from the rear gun turret, but the door remained jammed fast and the rear gunner could not get out.

The wireless operator appeared at this stage with fire extinguishers from the front of the aircraft. He went to tackle the incendiary kicked aside by Bridger, but as he did so four more incendiary bombs caught light and by their light the horrified men could see ten more on the fuselage floor. Bridger kicked all the lit incendiaries into a single spot on the fuselage floor and emptied extinguisher after extinguisher on to them while the wireless operator began dropping the bombs that had not yet ignited down the flare shute. By this time the entire fuselage was filled with acrid, choking smoke which blinded the two men. Working by touch alone, the two men managed to get the fires out, and the cold wind pouring in through the numerous holes in the fuselage dissipated the smoke.

Only then did Bridger report his paralysed leg and allow the wireless operator to examine it. Nothing seemed broken, though there was a large and livid red mark on the thigh. The wireless operator spent some time searching around the fuselage for other bombs, then helped Bridger limp back toward the cockpit. Though the fires were out, the dangers of night fighters remained. Bridger's turret was smashed, so he clambered up into the astrodome from where he could keep a look out for danger. The bomber got home without further incident, and apart from a massive bruise on Bridger's leg, nobody was injured.

Of the men who had flown with No.50 Squadron during the war, none had a more impressive post war career than Michael Beetham, the schoolboy

SIR ARTHUR HARRIS TRIBUTE, 1986
In 1986 the Royal Mail issued a special stamp to honour "Bomber" Harris. Even at this date Harris remained controversial as many blamed him for the high civilian casualties in Germany.

who had joined the RAF as ground crew before working his way up to be a Lancaster pilot. He stayed in the RAF when the war was over. After a series of promotions and staff appointments, Beetham was given command of the large air base at Khormaksar in Aden. No sooner had he arrived than the Aden Emergency broke out in December 1963. This struggle saw the British, as colonial power, pitted against a well funded guerrilla and terrorist insurgency fighting as much for Arab nationalism as for Islamic liberation. Beetham was responsible for security at Khormaksar and for ensuring that the nine squadrons based there were able to operate freely and effectively. He later went on to hold a series of senior staff positions, but No.50 Squadron had not yet heard the last of Beetham.

During the long years of conflict the men of No. 50 Squadron had been awarded many medals and decorations. Among these were Manser's Victoria Cross, 6 DSOs, 70 DFCs and 114 DFMs.

When the war ended, No.50 Squadron was moved from RAF Skellingthorpe to RAF Sturgate, where they would remain for a year before the station was closed for rebuilding to be suitable for jet aircraft. The squadron moved back to Waddington, where they had been reformed.

At Waddington the squadron was stripped of its Lancasters and instead acquired Avro Lincoln bombers. The Lincoln was a development of the Lancaster and had, at first, been designated the Lancaster Mk.IV. The Lincoln had extended wings and more powerful engines than the Lancaster, allowing it to fly higher and further than the bomber it replaced. Although the air forces of the world were entering the jet age, the performance and lifting ability of the Lincoln ensured that they remained in service. No.50 squadron kept them until it was disbanded in 1951.

Down to the Falklands

No 50 Squadron was re-formed at RAF Binbrook on 15 August 1952, where it was equipped with the English Electric Canberra light jet bomber. The Canberra was designed to be the RAF's first jet bomber and entered service as such in 1951, but it soon proved itself to be a highly adaptable and flexible design. It could reach 580mph and 48,000 feet, and had a combat range of over 800 miles. The aircraft was used in a variety of roles including bomber, nuclear bomber, high altitude spy aircraft, interdictor, electronic warfare carrier and a host of others. No.50 Squadron, however, used the bomber variant. The squadron moved to RAF

CANBERRA PR9, 1955
The Canberra was the first jet bomber to enter service with the RAF, and with No.50 Squadron. This version is a PR9 reconnoissance model used against the IRA and in Bosnia as well as against the Russians in the Cold War. (Photo: MilborneOne)

Upwood in Cambridgeshire in January 1956, and was disbanded there on 1 October 1959.

When the squadron was reformed again 1 August 1961 back at RAF Waddington it was as a V-bomber Squadron equipped with the mighty Vulcan bomber, another product of the Avro company.

The Vulcan entered service with the RAF and was constantly updated throughout its service life. Its initial purpose was to be a nuclear bomber, carrying nuclear bombs to distant targets in the days before missiles were reliably accurate. It had a cruising speed of 610mph and a top speed of 632mph, could reach 56,000 feet and had an impressive range of 4,600 miles. When not carrying a nuclear bomb it could carry 21,000lb of conventional bombs or other weaponry. The Vulcan proved to be an easy aircraft to fly and was surprisingly nimble in the air despite its huge size. It was not always a popular bomber with crews, however, as leaving the fuselage was not easy and in emergencies the delay in getting out could, and did, prove fatal to crew members.

The only time the Vulcan saw combat was during the Falklands War and No.50 Squadron was in the thick of the action. The Argentinian invasion of the islands in the South Atlantic on 2 April 1982 came as a surprise, and the British response had to be prepared in a great hurry. While the diplomats were seeking a peaceful solution – in vain as it transpired – and the Royal Navy was preparing its naval task force, the RAF had the tricky task of attacking targets on the island. The most important of these targets was the airport at Port Stanley that the Argentinian occupying force was using for supply purposes. Important though it was to cut the supply route, the airport represented an even greater danger as the long concrete runway could be used by Argentinian combat jets. If the Argentinian air force were to be able to operate from Port Stanley they would be able to achieve and hold air superiority over the islands, making any naval attack almost impossible.

On 25 April the first signs of a British armed response came when the outlying island of South Georgia was recaptured by naval forces, and an Argentinian submarine sunk. Then it was the turn of the RAF.

The tactical staff working on the problems of attacking the Falklands from the air had decided that the only feasible plan was to fly Vulcan bombers from Ascension Island. The bombers needed a long runway, and the nearest that could be used was on Ascension. The distance from Ascension to the Falklands was 4,000 miles, with another 4,000 miles back again, a total of 16 hours

119

flying time. That meant the Vulcans were still out of range of the Falklands, so they had to be refueled in the air from Handley Page Victor air tankers. Those aircraft had too limited a range to stooge about over the ocean waiting for the Vulcans, so they in turn had to be refuelled in the air from other Victors. Given the need for standby aircraft to act as back ups in an emergency, it meant that each Vulcan bomber needed five Victors in operation to get it to the Falklands and back. In addition to these technical issues, there was a political problem in that the airfield at Ascension Island was, although belonging to Britain, leased to the USA. A quick diplomatic exchange followed, and agreement was reached.

The Vulcan bombers had for some years been earmarked for use as medium-range bombers so, although there were equipped for air-to-air refuelling the equipment was in desperate need of repair and the crews were out of practice. Immediate training began at RAF Waddington to ensure the crews were adept at refuelling, while the maintenance teams began stripping down the systems on those aircraft that would be going south.

Intelligence reports indicated that the Argentinians had installed radar-guided Tigercat missiles and radar-controlled anti-aircraft guns around Port Stanley Airport. On missions over Europe, the Vulcans were to have been accompanied by ground-attack and electronic warfare aircraft to suppress defences, but over the Falklands they would be alone. To stand a chance of surviving their missions, the Vulcans had to be fitted with their own electronic warfare systems. The add-on chosen was the Dash 10, a sophisticated system that detected incoming radar pulses from radar-guided missiles and then distorted the reflected response to trick the missile into thinking that the targetted aircraft was a couple of miles away from where it actually was. The Dash 10 had to be mounted on an external pod if it was to be effective, but the Vulcans had no such attachments. Engineers at Waddington had to improvise by welding metal pylons on to the Vulcans.

Navigation across the vast featureless wastes of the South Atlantic was another problem. The navigational systems from commercial VC10 airliners were acquired on a temporary basis and fitted to the Vulcans. Unavoidably, much retraining of crews was needed to get them proficient in the use of Dash 10 and the new navigational equipment. An additional problem soon surfaced in that the reconfigured bomber was over its designed safe take off weight. The RAF decided to ignore the recommendation and carry on regardless.

AVRO VULCAN BOMBER, 1982

It was with the Vulcan that No.50 Squadron achieved its greatest post-1945 successes during the Falklands War. The Vulcan entered service in 1956 and remained the RAF's long range bomber to 1984.

On 30 April the first attack took off, using the code name of "Black Buck 1". Two Vulcans were involved, but XM598 flown by Squadron Leader John Reeve of No.50 Squadron suffered a sudden failure of pressurisation on the outward flight and returned to Ascension. XM607 piloted by Flight Lieutenant Martin Withers of No.101 Squadron flew on alone. The bombing raid took the Argentinians completely by surprise. They had assumed that no attacks would take place until the naval task force arrived with its aircraft carrier. The 21 1,000lb bombs caused extensive damage, including a near hit to the control tower, a direct hit on the runway and damage to a number of temporary structures put up by the Argentinian air force. The damage ensured that the airport could not be used by combat jets, at least not until it was repaired, but it remained open to transport aircraft and so Port Stanley Airport remained a key supply route for the Argentinian forces occupying the islands.

Black Buck 2 took off on 3 May, again aiming to bomb Port Stanley Airport out of operational condition. Squadron Leader John Reeve and his crew of No 50 Squadron this time completed the mission. They bombed the western end of the airport with the intention of destroying building works that were thought to be intended to extend the runway and provide the maintenence facilities needed if fast combat jets were to be based at Port Stanley. The aircraft came under unexpected fire from a surface to air missile

VULCAN XM597, 1982
Squadron Leader Neil McDougall of No.50
Squadron flew two bombing raids to Port Stanley
during the Falklands War in this Vulcan XM597. The
nose was painted with two missiles and a Brazilian
flag to symbolise the two raids and the internment
in Brazil.

(SAM), later identified as a Roland. This SAM was manufactured in France
for the export market and had been sold to Argentina some years earlier. It
had only a short range, but was considered to be highly effective and its
presence at Port Stanley came as a nasty surprise.

Black Buck 3 and Black Buck 4 were both cancelled due to adverse
weather conditions, but on 31 May Black Buck 5 went ahead. This mission,
flown by Squadron Leader Neil McDougall and his crew from 50 Squadron
in XM597, was designed to knock out the Argentinian air defences around
Port Stanley. For the attack the Vulcan was armed with AGM-45 Shrike
missiles that could home in on radar and other radio emissions. The primary
target was the AN-TPS-43 long range radar which the Argentinians were
using to detect the approach of the Vulcans, and would soon be wanting to

use against British naval aircraft. For the Shrikes to work, the target radar had to be switched on. As McDougall approached Port Stanley his crew picked up the signals from the AN-TPS-43 and McDougall launched his first Shrike. Neither he nor anybody else on board had ever fired a Shrike before and they nervously awaited the outcome. They monitored the missile as it homed in on the ground radar, struck and exploded. The AN-TPS-43 promptly shut down. Believing he had destroyed his target, McDougall headed home.

In fact the Shrike had struck the ground 30 feet from the radar. The blast had inflicted a fair degree of damage to the Argentinian radar, but had not destroyed it. After some repair work, the AN-TPS-43 was up and running by nightfall the following day.

On 3 June, McDougall and his crew returned to the attack. Believing the AN-TPS-43 was knocked out, they this time had as their primary target the short range Skyguard radar that controlled the anti-aircraft guns at Port Stanley. This time things did not go according to plan. When the AN-TPS-43 picked up the Vulcan, the Skyguard was switched off, thus making it invisible to the Shrike guidance system. McDougall was, however, equal to the task. The Vulcan is a large aircraft, but because of its shape it can from some angles give a radar response much smaller than its actual size. In the days before stealth technology this fact was not appreciated by most defenders, and McDougall sought to take advantage of this fact.

McDougall knew that the Argentinians were aware of the critical fuel problems of Vulcans operating at such a vast range from their base. A Vulcan loaded down with 21 1,000lb bombs had time for only one bombing run before it had to turn back. But McDougall had the much lighter Shrikes, so he had a wide margin of error for fuel usage. He flew back out to sea as if returning to base. Once out of radar range of Port Stanley, he then swung round to approach the land again, but this time behaving as if he were a small jet flown from an aircraft carrier. These jets did not routinely carry Shrikes. McDougall was gambling that the defenders would mistake him for a follow-up attack by a small jet and switch on the Skyguard. The ruse worked, the Skyguard was detected and the Shrike fired. This time there was no error and the target was utterly destroyed.

McDougall then really did turn for home. Even now, however, his adventures were not over. High over the South Atlantic he met up with the Victor refuelling tanker, but during refuelling the probe on the Vulcan snapped off. McDougall did not have enough fuel to get to Ascension Island.

The only airport within range that had a runway long enough for the Vulcan, and which was not in Argentina, was Rio de Janeiro in Brazil. McDougal sent out a standard Mayday signal informing the Brazilian authorities that he needed to make an emergency landing and was critically short of fuel. Meanwhile, he ordered his crew to dump out of the escape hatch all documents relating to their mission, to their squadron and to Ascension Island.

Brazil was known to be sympathetic to the Argentinian cause. They had loaned maritime patrol aircraft to the Argentinian airforce. Not only that, but a diplomatic incident between Britain and Brazil had erupted on 23 April when a Brazilian commercial airliner flying from Rio to Cape Town had strayed off its route and come close to the Royal Navy task force steaming south. British fighters scrambled from the aircraft carrier HMS Invincible had intercepted the airliner and escorted it away from the task force. Whether the incident had been accidental, or if the airliner had deliberately sought to overfly the task force was never clear, but the military interception of a civilian airliner caused a bit of a fuss.

McDougall was, therefore, entirely uncertain what sort of reception he would get at Rio. He tried to dump his spare Shrike into the sea, but it refused to leave the Vulcan. As the bomber approached Brazil it became alarmingly clear to McDougall that his fuel was so low that he would have to land on his first approach, there being not enough fuel to do a circuit and try again. McDougall alerted the Rio control tower, with the result that the runway was cleared, the aircraft waiting to land ordered to fly away from the airport and emergency services on the ground got ready for a crash.

In the event the landing went perfectly. The Brazilian authorities were all smiles, and welcomed McDougall and his crew with open arms. They were whisked off to nearby Galeão Air Force Base where they were given a hot meal, private rooms and bathing facilities. Rather more ominously, the Vulcan was sealed off from prying eyes by the Brazilian military. While McDougall and the other men from No.50 Squadron were being entertained most charmingly at Galeão, the diplomats got to work to try to arrange the repatriation of the crew and the Vulcan. The Brazilians were all smiles and declared themselves willing to expedite things as quickly as possible, though there then occurred some unexplained delays. In the end it was nine days before McDougall was reunited with his Vulcan and allowed to fly off for Ascension Island. Unsurprisingly there were signs that the Brazilians had been all over the aircraft, inspecting and examining everything they could lay their hands on. Rather less expected was the fact that the spare Shrike was missing. The Brazilians shrugged their shoulders and denied all knowledge. What had happened to it has never been firmly established, but there can be little doubt that the Brazilians had decided to keep it for themselves.

A final Black Buck mission was flown by Withers on 12 June, just two days before the Argentinian forces on the Falklands surrendered to the ground forces landed from the naval task force.

The effectiveness of the Black Buck raids has long been a source of controversy. The apparently small scale damage inflicted on the ground has led some to suggest that they were something of a failure. In fact the missions not only achieved their stated aims, but had some unforseen advantages as well.

The primary aim of the raids was to ensure that Port Stanly Airport could not be used by Argentinian fast military jets. If it had been, then the Argentinians would have been able to secure air superiority over the islands, and a British naval landing would have been almost impossible. This aim was

ROLAND SAM, 1982
The Argentinians protected Stanley Airfield with French-built Roland surface-to-air missiles. Eight of the ten missiles were fired, bringing down one British Harrier jump jet.

achieved completely. The Argentinians had installed arrestor wires on the runway ready for the arrival of Skyhawk jets, but after Black Buck 1 the deployment was cancelled.

The raids also served as an early and very clear signal that Britain was going to fight for the Falklands and was determined to do whatever was necessary to win. In the weeks after the Argentinian invasion while the naval task force was being prepared and was steaming south, the opinion had grown in many countries that Britain would settle for a compromise negotiated peace. The Argentine military government led by General Galtieri had hardened its stance in diplomatic talks on this very assumption. Black Buck showed the determination of the British government of Mrs Thatcher to get the islands back without compromise.

Quite unintended was the effect that the raids had on the plans of the Argentinian military. After Black Buck 1 Vice Admiral Jouan Lombardo, who was in charge of Argentinian naval operations, came to the conclusion that the British task force was about to make a dash for the Falklands and land their

AGM-45 SHRIKE ON CART, 1982
The Vulcan of No.50 Squadron that attacked the Argentinians on the Falklands was armed with Shrike missiles, designed to home in on and destroy radar installations.

troops at Port Stanley. This was not the British plan, but Lombardo ordered a hastily conceived and poorly planned naval assault on the task force under this misapprehension. He ordered his own aircraft carrier led task force to attack the British from the north while his big gun cruiser, the General Belgrano, with its escort ships swept up from the south.

The Argentinian naval moves were detected by the British and on 2 May the Belgrano was sunk by the British submarine HMS Conqueror. The cruiser sank along with 323 of her crew. The Argentinian navy then withdrew to port and played no further part in the war. The British naval task force had thus been cleared of a serious worry.

Also unexpected was that the Argentinians withdrew a number of their jets, operating from mainland bases, from the growing air battle over the islands. The Argentinians believed that the British were going to launch Vulcan bombing attacks on their military bases on the Argentinian mainland, and so held back fighters to defend those targets. The British had no intention of mounting such attacks since the politicians had decided that direct attacks on Argentina would needlessly escalate the war that was being fought solely to regain control of the Falklands.

The runway did remain in use during the war despite the damage done to it. Smaller Argentinian aircraft such as the ground-attack Pucara operated out of Port Stanley right up to the surrender. However, the airport had ceased to be a source of large scale supplies to the Argentinians long before this.

During the Falklands War, the Chief of the Defence Staff was none other than the old No.50 Squadron pilot and veteran of the Battle of Britain Michael Beetham. His role in organising the Falklands Task Force was immense and much of the credit for the success of the war was his. After the Falklands War, Beetham was promoted to the exalted rank of Marshal of the Royal Air Force, and then retired. As a special mark of honour he was allowed to remain on the Active List, though his main service is to support the work of the RAF Museum at Hendon. In 2005 Beetham clambered aboard a Lancaster one more time to take part in the fly past over London to mark the 60th Anniversary of the end of World War II.

By the time Beetham was flying over London in the Lancaster operated by the RAF Battle of Britain Memorial Flight, his old squadron was no more. No.50 Squadron was disbanded at RAF Waddington on 31 March 1984, the same date on which the Vulcan bomber was retired from service. The long and glorious history of No.50 Squadron was over. For now.